COMMON CORE
SKILLS & STRATEGIES FOR VOCABULARY

Level 7

COMMON CORE
SKILLS & STRATEGIES FOR VOCABULARY

Level 3
Level 4
Level 5
Level 6
Level 7
Level 8

© 2004, 2014 by Saddleback Educational Publishing
All rights reserved. No part of this book may be reproduced in any form or by any means, electronic or mechanical, including photocopying, recording, scanning, or by any information storage and retrieval system, without the written permission of the publisher. SADDLEBACK EDUCATIONAL PUBLISHING and any associated logos are trademarks and/or registered trademarks of Saddleback Educational Publishing.

Pages labeled with the statement © Saddleback Educational Publishing are intended for reproduction. Saddleback Publishing, Inc. grants to individual purchasers of this book the right to make sufficient copies of reproducible pages for use by all students of a single teacher. This permission is limited to a single teacher, and does not apply to entire schools or school systems.

ISBN-13: 978-1-62250-907-2
ISBN-10: 1-62250-907-2
eBook: 978-1-63078-023-4

Printed in the United States of America
18 17 16 15 14   1 2 3 4 5

Table of Contents
Skills

Teacher welcome and tips vi	Adverbs: Getting Meaning from Context Clues 23
Common Core Alignment chart viii	Forms of a Word: Adjective to Noun 1 24
English Vocabularies: Formal, Informal, and Slang 1 2	Forms of a Word: Adjective to Noun 2 25
English Vocabularies: Formal, Informal, and Slang 2 3	Forms of a Word: Verb to Adjective 1 26
Using the Dictionary 1 4	Forms of a Word: Verb to Adjective 2 27
Using the Dictionary 2 5	Forms of a Word: Noun to Verb 1 28
Information in a Dictionary Entry 1 6	Forms of a Word: Noun to Verb 2 29
Information in a Dictionary Entry 2 7	Just for Fun: Word Ladders 1 30
Denotation and Connotation 1 8	Just for Fun: Word Ladders 2 31
Denotation and Connotation 2 9	Making Compound Words 1 32
Just for Fun: Dictionary Challenge 1 10	Making Compound Words 2 33
Just for Fun: Dictionary Challenge 2 11	Compound Words: *Head* and *Foot* 1 34
Pronunciation: Vowel Sounds 1 12	Compound Words: *Head* and *Foot* 2 35
Pronunciation: Vowel Sounds 2 13	Compound Words: *Air* and *Water* 1 36
Pronunciation: Silent Letters 1 14	Compound Words: *Air* and *Water* 2 37
Pronunciation: Silent Letters 2 15	Compound Words: *Sun* and *Wind* 1 38
Pronunciation: Syllables and Accent Marks 1 16	Compound Words: *Sun* and *Wind* 2 39
Pronunciation: Syllables and Accent Marks 2 17	Choosing Precise Words 1 40
Using Context Clues 1 18	Choosing Precise Words 2 41
Using Context Clues 2 19	Greek Roots 1 42
Nouns: Getting Meaning from Context Clues 20	Greek Roots 2 43
Verbs: Getting Meaning from Context Clues 21	Latin Roots 1 44
Adjectives: Getting Meaning from Context Clues 22	Latin Roots 2 45
	Prefixes 1 46
	Prefixes 2 47
	Suffixes 1 48

Suffixes 2	49
Near Misses 1	50
Near Misses 2	51
Synonyms: Nouns 1	52
Synonyms: Nouns 2	53
Synonyms: Verbs 1	54
Synonyms: Verbs 2	55
Synonyms: Adjectives 1	56
Synonyms: Adjectives 2	57
Synonyms: Adverbs 1	58
Synonyms: Adverbs 2	59
Antonyms: Nouns 1	60
Antonyms: Nouns 2	61
Antonyms: Verbs 1	62
Antonyms: Verbs 2	63
Antonyms: Adjectives 1	64
Antonyms: Adjectives 2	65
Antonyms: Adverbs 1	66
Antonyms: Adverbs 2	67
Homophones	68
Homophone Riddles	69
Homographs	70
Homophones and Homographs: Dictionary Practice	71
Clipped Words 1	72
Clipped Words 2	73
Words Borrowed from Names 1	74
Words Borrowed from Names 2	75
Foreign Words and Phrases 1	76
Foreign Words and Phrases 2	77
Simple Idioms 1	78
Simple Idioms 2	79
Interpreting Idioms 1	80
Interpreting Idioms 2	81
Explaining Idioms 1	82
Explaining Idioms 2	83
Using Idioms in Context 1	84
Using Idioms in Context 2	85
A-B Words in Context 1	86
A-B Words in Context 2	87
C-D Words in Context 1	88
C-D Words in Context 2	89
E-F Words in Context 1	90
E-F Words in Context 2	91
G-H Words in Context 1	92
G-H Words in Context 2	93
I-J Words in Context 1	94
I-J Words in Context 2	95
K-L Words in Context 1	96
K-L Words in Context 2	97
M-N Words in Context 1	98
M-N Words in Context 2	99
O-P Words in Context 1	100
O-P Words in Context 2	101
Q-R Words in Context 1	102
Q-R Words in Context 2	103
S-T Words in Context 1	104
S-T Words in Context 2	105
U-V Words in Context 1	106

U-V Words in Context 2 107

W-X Words in Context 1 108

W-X Words in Context 2 109

Y-Z Words in Context 1 110

Y-Z Words in Context 2 111

Just for Fun: Explaining Why
  or Why Not 112

Just for Fun: Exploring Big Words 113

Shopping Words 1 114

Shopping Words 2 115

Law Words 1 116

Law Words 2 117

Building Words 1 118

Building Words 2 119

Space Words 1 120

Space Words 2 121

Health Words 1 122

Health Words 2 123

Business Words 1 124

Business Words 2 125

Travel Words 1 126

Travel Words 2 127

Government Words 1 128

Government Words 2 129

Party Words 1 130

Party Words 2 131

Scope and Sequence 132

Answer Key 134

Welcome to
Common Core Skills & Strategies for Vocabulary

About This Series

The Common Core State Standards (CCSS) provide a consistent, clear understanding of what students are expected to learn in the area of vocabulary acquisition and use, a key component to literacy. Aligning each lesson in these six Common Core titles to the CCSS English language arts standards ensures that students are being exposed to grade-level content. The alignment helps educators think critically about their curriculum, instruction, and assessments as they work to ensure that their students meet the rigorous new standards.

Beginning with foundational skills, the activities teach students in a balanced and methodical way. The alignments offer a progressive development of vocabulary acquisition and use so that students advancing through the levels are able to gain more from whatever they read. Each title includes a table of contents, a CCSS alignment chart, 130 reproducible lessons individually aligned to the CCSS (each lesson contains a discrete alignment at the bottom of the page), a scope and sequence chart, and an answer key.

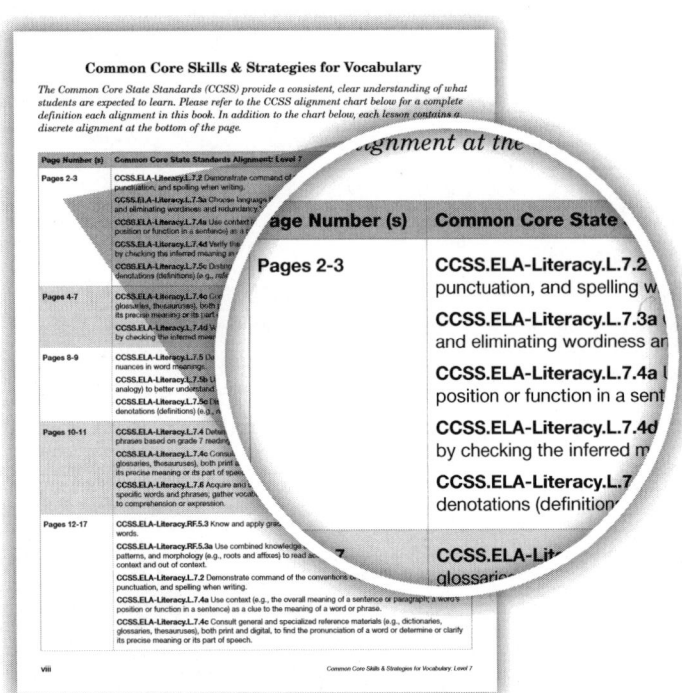

CCSS Alignment Chart

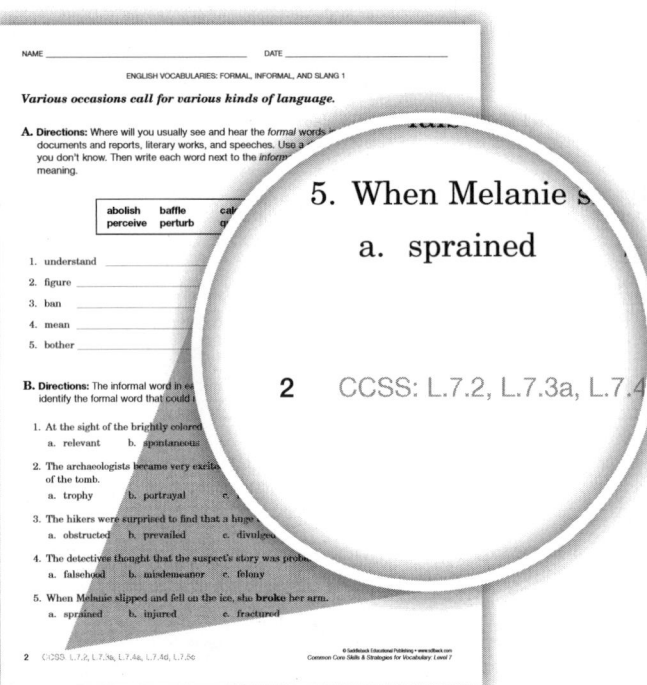

Discrete Alignment on Each Page

About This Book

Common Core Skills and Strategies for Vocabulary is designed to build your students' word power in short incremental lessons, providing you with maximum flexibility in deciding when and how to use these exercises. All-important concepts—ranging from primary-level phonics to the nuances of connotation—are thoroughly presented. Traditional word attack strategies and "getting meaning from context clues" are dually emphasized. Aligning each lesson in these six Common Core titles to the CCSS English language arts standards ensures that students are being exposed to grade-level content. The alignment helps educators think critically about their curriculum, instruction, and assessments as they work to ensure that their students meet the rigorous new standards.

Each book includes a CD, which contains a complete electronic version of the reproducible as an "Unlocked PDF." Unlocked PDFs allow users to copy/paste text and certain images for posting, emailing, projecting on a whiteboard, and more.

Choosing Instructional Approaches

You can use the pages in this book for independent reinforcement or extension, whole group lessons, pairs, or small cooperative groups rotating through an established reading learning center. You may choose to place the activities in a center and reproduce the answer key for self-checking. To ensure the utmost flexibility, the process for managing this is left entirely up to you because you know what works best in your classroom.

Assessment

Assessment and evaluation of student understanding and ability is an ongoing process. A variety of methods and strategies should be used to ensure that the student is being assessed and evaluated in a fair and comprehensive manner. Always keep in mind that the assessment should take into consideration the opportunities the student had to learn the information and practice the skills presented. The strategies for assessment are left for you to determine and are dependent on your students and your particular instructional plan. You will find a Scope and Sequence Chart at the back of this book to assist you as you develop your assessment plan.

Common Core Skills & Strategies for Vocabulary

The Common Core State Standards (CCSS) provide a consistent, clear understanding of what students are expected to learn. Please refer to the CCSS alignment chart below for a complete definition each alignment in this book. In addition to the chart below, each lesson contains a discrete alignment at the bottom of the page.

Page Number (s)	Common Core State Standards Alignment: Level 7
Pages 2-3	**CCSS.ELA-Literacy.L.7.2** Demonstrate command of the conventions of standard English capitalization, punctuation, and spelling when writing. **CCSS.ELA-Literacy.L.7.3a** Choose language that expresses ideas precisely and concisely, recognizing and eliminating wordiness and redundancy.* **CCSS.ELA-Literacy.L.7.4a** Use context (e.g., the overall meaning of a sentence or paragraph; a word's position or function in a sentence) as a clue to the meaning of a word or phrase. **CCSS.ELA-Literacy.L.7.4d** Verify the preliminary determination of the meaning of a word or phrase (e.g., by checking the inferred meaning in context or in a dictionary). **CCSS.ELA-Literacy.L.7.5c** Distinguish among the connotations (associations) of words with similar denotations (definitions) (e.g., *refined, respectful, polite, diplomatic, condescending*).
Pages 4-7	**CCSS.ELA-Literacy.L.7.4c** Consult general and specialized reference materials (e.g., dictionaries, glossaries, thesauruses), both print and digital, to find the pronunciation of a word or determine or clarify its precise meaning or its part of speech. **CCSS.ELA-Literacy.L.7.4d** Verify the preliminary determination of the meaning of a word or phrase (e.g., by checking the inferred meaning in context or in a dictionary).
Pages 8-9	**CCSS.ELA-Literacy.L.7.5** Demonstrate understanding of figurative language, word relationships, and nuances in word meanings. **CCSS.ELA-Literacy.L.7.5b** Use the relationship between particular words (e.g., synonym/antonym, analogy) to better understand each of the words. **CCSS.ELA-Literacy.L.7.5c** Distinguish among the connotations (associations) of words with similar denotations (definitions) (e.g., *refined, respectful, polite, diplomatic, condescending*).
Pages 10-11	**CCSS.ELA-Literacy.L.7.4** Determine or clarify the meaning of unknown and multiple-meaning words and phrases based on grade 7 reading and content, choosing flexibly from a range of strategies. **CCSS.ELA-Literacy.L.7.4c** Consult general and specialized reference materials (e.g., dictionaries, glossaries, thesauruses), both print and digital, to find the pronunciation of a word or determine or clarify its precise meaning or its part of speech. **CCSS.ELA-Literacy.L.7.6** Acquire and use accurately grade-appropriate general academic and domain-specific words and phrases; gather vocabulary knowledge when considering a word or phrase important to comprehension or expression.
Pages 12-17	**CCSS.ELA-Literacy.RF.5.3** Know and apply grade-level phonics and word analysis skills in decoding words. **CCSS.ELA-Literacy.RF.5.3a** Use combined knowledge of all letter-sound correspondences, syllabication patterns, and morphology (e.g., roots and affixes) to read accurately unfamiliar multisyllabic words in context and out of context. **CCSS.ELA-Literacy.L.7.2** Demonstrate command of the conventions of standard English capitalization, punctuation, and spelling when writing. **CCSS.ELA-Literacy.L.7.4a** Use context (e.g., the overall meaning of a sentence or paragraph; a word's position or function in a sentence) as a clue to the meaning of a word or phrase. **CCSS.ELA-Literacy.L.7.4c** Consult general and specialized reference materials (e.g., dictionaries, glossaries, thesauruses), both print and digital, to find the pronunciation of a word or determine or clarify its precise meaning or its part of speech.

Page Number (s)	Common Core State Standards Alignment: Level 7
Pages 18-19	**CCSS.ELA-Literacy.L.7.3** Use knowledge of language and its conventions when writing, speaking, reading, or listening. **CCSS.ELA-Literacy.L.7.4** Determine or clarify the meaning of unknown and multiple-meaning words and phrases based on grade 7 reading and content, choosing flexibly from a range of strategies. **CCSS.ELA-Literacy.L.7.4a** Use context (e.g., the overall meaning of a sentence or paragraph; a word's position or function in a sentence) as a clue to the meaning of a word or phrase. **CCSS.ELA-Literacy.L.7.4b** Use common, grade-appropriate Greek or Latin affixes and roots as clues to the meaning of a word (e.g., belligerent, bellicose, rebel). **CCSS.ELA-Literacy.L.7.4c** Consult general and specialized reference materials (e.g., dictionaries, glossaries, thesauruses), both print and digital, to find the pronunciation of a word or determine or clarify its precise meaning or its part of speech.
Pages 20-23	**CCSS.ELA-Literacy.L.7.1** Demonstrate command of the conventions of standard English grammar and usage when writing or speaking. **CCSS.ELA-Literacy.L.7.4a** Use context (e.g., the overall meaning of a sentence or paragraph; a word's position or function in a sentence) as a clue to the meaning of a word or phrase. **CCSS.ELA-Literacy.L.7.4c** Consult general and specialized reference materials (e.g., dictionaries, glossaries, thesauruses), both print and digital, to find the pronunciation of a word or determine or clarify its precise meaning or its part of speech. **CCSS.ELA-Literacy.L.7.2b** Spell correctly.
Pages 24-29	**CCSS.ELA-Literacy.L.7.1** Demonstrate command of the conventions of standard English grammar and usage when writing or speaking. **CCSS.ELA-Literacy.L.7.3** Use knowledge of language and its conventions when writing, speaking, reading, or listening. **CCSS.ELA-Literacy.L.7.4d** Verify the preliminary determination of the meaning of a word or phrase (e.g., by checking the inferred meaning in context or in a dictionary). **CCSS.ELA-Literacy.W.7.2d** Use precise language and domain-specific vocabulary to inform about or explain the topic.
Pages 30-31	**CCSS.ELA-Literacy.RF.5.3** Know and apply grade-level phonics and word analysis skills in decoding words. **CCSS.ELA-Literacy.L.7.2** Demonstrate command of the conventions of standard English capitalization, punctuation, and spelling when writing.
Pages 32-39	**CCSS.ELA-Literacy.L.7.4** Determine or clarify the meaning of unknown and multiple-meaning words and phrases based on *grade 7 reading and content*, choosing flexibly from a range of strategies. **CCSS.ELA-Literacy.L.7.4a** Use context (e.g., the overall meaning of a sentence or paragraph; a word's position or function in a sentence) as a clue to the meaning of a word or phrase. **CCSS.ELA-Literacy.L.7.3** Use knowledge of language and its conventions when writing, speaking, reading, or listening. **CCSS.ELA-Literacy.L.7.5** Demonstrate understanding of figurative language, **word relationships**, and nuances in word meanings.

Page Number (s)	Common Core State Standards Alignment: Level 7
Pages 40-41	**CCSS.ELA-Literacy.L.7.3** Use knowledge of language and its conventions when writing, speaking, reading, or listening. **CCSS.ELA-Literacy.L.7.3a** Choose language that expresses ideas precisely and concisely, recognizing and eliminating wordiness and redundancy.* **CCSS.ELA-Literacy.L.7.5** Demonstrate understanding of figurative language, word relationships, and nuances in word meanings. **CCSS.ELA-Literacy.L.7.5b** Use the relationship between particular words (e.g., synonym/antonym, analogy) to better understand each of the words. **CCSS.ELA-Literacy.W.7.2d** Use precise language and domain-specific vocabulary to inform about or explain the topic.
Pages 42-49	**CCSS.ELA-Literacy.L.7.2b** Spell correctly. **CCSS.ELA-Literacy.L.7.4** Determine or clarify the meaning of unknown and multiple-meaning words and phrases based on *grade 7 reading and content,* choosing flexibly from a range of strategies. **CCSS.ELA-Literacy.L.7.4a** Use context (e.g., the overall meaning of a sentence or paragraph; a word's position or function in a sentence) as a clue to the meaning of a word or phrase. **CCSS.ELA-Literacy.L.7.4b** Use common, grade-appropriate Greek or Latin affixes and roots as clues to the meaning of a word (e.g., *belligerent, bellicose, rebel*). **CCSS.ELA-Literacy.L.7.6** Acquire and use accurately grade-appropriate general academic and domain-specific words and phrases; gather vocabulary knowledge when considering a word or phrase important to comprehension or expression.
Pages 50-51	**CCSS.ELA-Literacy.L.7.3** Use knowledge of language and its conventions when writing, speaking, reading, or listening. **CCSS.ELA-Literacy.L.7.4a** Use context (e.g., the overall meaning of a sentence or paragraph; a word's position or function in a sentence) as a clue to the meaning of a word or phrase.
Pages 52-59	**CCSS.ELA-Literacy.L.7.1** Demonstrate command of the conventions of standard English grammar and usage when writing or speaking. **CCSS.ELA-Literacy.L.7.2b** Spell correctly. **CCSS.ELA-Literacy.L.7.4a** Use context (e.g., the overall meaning of a sentence or paragraph; a word's position or function in a sentence) as a clue to the meaning of a word or phrase. **CCSS.ELA-Literacy.L.7.4c** Consult general and specialized reference materials (e.g., dictionaries, glossaries, thesauruses), both print and digital, to find the pronunciation of a word or determine or clarify its precise meaning or its part of speech. **CCSS.ELA-Literacy.L.7.5b** Use the relationship between particular words (e.g., synonym/antonym, analogy) to better understand each of the words. **CCSS.ELA-Literacy.L.7.5c** Distinguish among the connotations (associations) of words with similar denotations (definitions) (e.g., *refined, respectful, polite, diplomatic, condescending*). **CCSS.ELA-Literacy.W.7.2d** Use precise language and domain-specific vocabulary to inform about or explain the topic.
Pages 60-67	**CCSS.ELA-Literacy.L.7.1** Demonstrate command of the conventions of standard English grammar and usage when writing or speaking. **CCSS.ELA-Literacy.L.7.2b** Spell correctly. **CCSS.ELA-Literacy.L.7.4a** Use context (e.g., the overall meaning of a sentence or paragraph; a word's position or function in a sentence) as a clue to the meaning of a word or phrase. **CCSS.ELA-Literacy.L.7.5b** Use the relationship between particular words (e.g., synonym/antonym, analogy) to better understand each of the words.

Page Number (s)	Common Core State Standards Alignment: Level 7
Pages 68-71	**CCSS.ELA-Literacy.L.7.3** Use knowledge of language and its conventions when writing, speaking, reading, or listening. **CCSS.ELA-Literacy.L.7.4a** Use context (e.g., the overall meaning of a sentence or paragraph; a word's position or function in a sentence) as a clue to the meaning of a word or phrase. **CCSS.ELA-Literacy.L.7.6** Acquire and use accurately grade-appropriate general academic and domain-specific words and phrases; gather vocabulary knowledge when considering a word or phrase important to comprehension or expression.
Pages 72-73	**CCSS.ELA-Literacy.L.7.3** Use knowledge of language and its conventions when writing, speaking, reading, or listening. **CCSS.ELA-Literacy.L.7.4a** Use context (e.g., the overall meaning of a sentence or paragraph; a word's position or function in a sentence) as a clue to the meaning of a word or phrase. **CCSS.ELA-Literacy.L.7.4c** Consult general and specialized reference materials (e.g., dictionaries, glossaries, thesauruses), both print and digital, to find the pronunciation of a word or determine or clarify its precise meaning or its part of speech. **CCSS.ELA-Literacy.L.7.6** Acquire and use accurately grade-appropriate general academic and domain-specific words and phrases; gather vocabulary knowledge when considering a word or phrase important to comprehension or expression.
Pages 74-75	**CCSS.ELA-Literacy.L.7.4c** Consult general and specialized reference materials (e.g., dictionaries, glossaries, thesauruses), both print and digital, to find the pronunciation of a word or determine or clarify its precise meaning or its part of speech. **CCSS.ELA-Literacy.RH.6-8.4** Determine the meaning of words and phrases as they are used in a text, including vocabulary specific to domains related to history/social studies.
Pages 76-77	**CCSS.ELA-Literacy.L.7.4** Determine or clarify the meaning of unknown and multiple-meaning words and phrases based on *grade 7 reading and content*, choosing flexibly from a range of strategies. **CCSS.ELA-Literacy.L.7.4a** Use context (e.g., the overall meaning of a sentence or paragraph; a word's position or function in a sentence) as a clue to the meaning of a word or phrase.
Pages 78-85	**CCSS.ELA-Literacy.L.7.4** Determine or clarify the meaning of unknown and multiple-meaning words and phrases based on *grade 7 reading and content*, choosing flexibly from a range of strategies. **CCSS.ELA-Literacy.L.7.4a** Use context (e.g., the overall meaning of a sentence or paragraph; a word's position or function in a sentence) as a clue to the meaning of a word or phrase. **CCSS.ELA-Literacy.L.7.5** Demonstrate understanding of figurative language, word relationships, and nuances in word meanings. **CCSS.ELA-Literacy.L.7.5a** Interpret figures of speech **CCSS.ELA-Literacy.L.7.6** Acquire and use accurately grade-appropriate general academic and domain-specific words and phrases; gather vocabulary knowledge when considering a word or phrase important to comprehension or expression.

Page Number (s)	Common Core State Standards Alignment: Level 7
Pages 86-111	**CCSS.ELA-Literacy.L.7.4** Determine or clarify the meaning of unknown and multiple-meaning words and phrases based on *grade 7 reading and content*, choosing flexibly from a range of strategies.
CCSS.ELA-Literacy.L.7.4a Use context (e.g., the overall meaning of a sentence or paragraph; a word's position or function in a sentence) as a clue to the meaning of a word or phrase.
CCSS.ELA-Literacy.L.7.4b Use common, grade-appropriate Greek or Latin affixes and roots as clues to the meaning of a word (e.g., *belligerent, bellicose, rebel*).
CCSS.ELA-Literacy.L.7.4c Consult general and specialized reference materials (e.g., dictionaries, glossaries, thesauruses), both print and digital, to find the pronunciation of a word or determine or clarify its precise meaning or its part of speech.
CCSS.ELA-Literacy.L.7.4d Verify the preliminary determination of the meaning of a word or phrase (e.g., by checking the inferred meaning in context or in a dictionary).
CCSS.ELA-Literacy.L.7.6 Acquire and use accurately grade-appropriate general academic and domain-specific words and phrases; gather vocabulary knowledge when considering a word or phrase important to comprehension or expression.
CCSS.ELA-Literacy.W.7.4 Produce clear and coherent writing in which the development, organization, and style are appropriate to task, purpose, and audience.
Pages 112-113	**CCSS.ELA-Literacy.L.7.4** Determine or clarify the meaning of unknown and multiple-meaning words and phrases based on *grade 7 reading and content,* choosing flexibly from a range of strategies.
CCSS.ELA-Literacy.L.7.4a Use context (e.g., the overall meaning of a sentence or paragraph; a word's position or function in a sentence) as a clue to the meaning of a word or phrase.
CCSS.ELA-Literacy.L.7.4b Use common, grade-appropriate Greek or Latin affixes and roots as clues to the meaning of a word (e.g., *belligerent, bellicose, rebel*).
CCSS.ELA-Literacy.L.7.4c Consult general and specialized reference materials (e.g., dictionaries, glossaries, thesauruses), both print and digital, to find the pronunciation of a word or determine or clarify its precise meaning or its part of speech.
CCSS.ELA-Literacy.L.7.6 Acquire and use accurately grade-appropriate general academic and domain-specific words and phrases; gather vocabulary knowledge when considering a word or phrase important to comprehension or expression.
Pages 114-131	**CCSS.ELA-Literacy.L.7.2b** Spell correctly.
CCSS.ELA-Literacy.L.7.4 Determine or clarify the meaning of unknown and multiple-meaning words and phrases based on *grade 7 reading and content*, choosing flexibly from a range of strategies.
CCSS.ELA-Literacy.L.7.4a Use context (e.g., the overall meaning of a sentence or paragraph; a word's position or function in a sentence) as a clue to the meaning of a word or phrase.
CCSS.ELA-Literacy.L.7.5 Demonstrate understanding of figurative language, **word relationships**, and nuances in word meanings.
CCSS.ELA-Literacy.L.7.5b Use the relationship between particular words (e.g., synonym/antonym, analogy) to better understand each of the words.
CCSS.ELA-Literacy.RH.6-8.4 Determine the meaning of words and phrases as they are used in a text, including vocabulary specific to domains related to history/social studies.
CCSS.ELA-Literacy.RST.6-8.4 Determine the meaning of symbols, key terms, and other domain-specific words and phrases as they are used in a specific scientific or technical context relevant to *grades 6–8 texts and topics*.

NAME _____ DATE _____

ENGLISH VOCABULARIES: FORMAL, INFORMAL, AND SLANG 1

Various occasions call for various kinds of language.

A. Directions: Where will you usually see and hear the *formal* words in the box? In official documents and reports, literary works, and speeches. Use a dictionary to look up any words you don't know. Then write each word next to the *informal* word below that has the same meaning.

| abolish | baffle | calculate | massive | notable |
| perceive | perturb | quest | signify | tedious |

1. understand _____
2. figure _____
3. ban _____
4. mean _____
5. bother _____
6. huge _____
7. confuse _____
8. famous _____
9. boring _____
10. search _____

B. Directions: The informal word in each sentence appears in **boldface**. Circle a letter to identify the formal word that could replace it.

1. At the sight of the brightly colored balloons, the child broke into a **sudden** smile.
   a. relevant   b. spontaneous   c. delirious

2. The archaeologists became very excited when they saw the **writing** on the walls of the tomb.
   a. trophy   b. portrayal   c. inscription

3. The hikers were surprised to find that a huge boulder **barred** their path.
   a. obstructed   b. prevailed   c. divulged

4. The detectives thought that the suspect's story was probably a **lie**.
   a. falsehood   b. misdemeanor   c. felony

5. When Melanie slipped and fell on the ice, she **broke** her arm.
   a. sprained   b. injured   c. fractured

NAME _____ DATE _____

ENGLISH VOCABULARIES: FORMAL, INFORMAL, AND SLANG 2

Informal *English is the language used in newspapers, on television, and in most everyday conversations.*

When talking to friends, most people use some slang expressions. Slang might be vivid and interesting in speech, but it is not acceptable in formal or informal writing.

A. Directions: Write a slang expression from the box that has the same meaning as the **boldface** word or words. Hint: You will not use all the words in the box.

| hangout | bimbo | batty | handle | bugs | chill | sleazy | ditzy |

1. "Slim" was given that **nickname** _____ about 10 years ago.
2. My dad always **pesters** _____ me about doing my homework.
3. Her high-pitched laugh makes her sound **silly** _____.
4. Sara suggested that we stop working and **relax** _____ for a while.
5. That rundown _____ neighborhood looks very **unappealing**.
6. The burger place was a favorite **gathering place** _____ for kids from our school.
7. Our **eccentric** _____ neighbor needs help from a psychiatrist.

B. Directions: Use vowels (*a, e, i, o, u*) to complete the words in the chart that have the same meaning.

FORMAL	INFORMAL	SLANG
1. m_e_l_a_n c h_o_l y	➡ sad	➡ down
2. vulgar	➡ c h_e a_p	➡ tacky
3. _o_b s_e_r v_e_	➡ see	➡ eyeball
4. genteel	➡ r_e_f_i_n_e_d	➡ high-toned
5. converse	➡ talk	➡ g_a_b
6. slander	➡ insult	➡ d_i s

NAME _____ DATE _____

USING THE DICTIONARY 1

The quickest source of information about words is the dictionary.

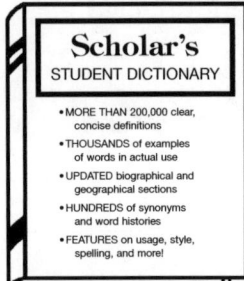

Here's one way to make it easier to use a dictionary. Think of a dictionary as being divided into three parts, or sections.

| A B C D E | F G H I J K L M N O P | Q R S T U V W X Y Z |

Flip the pages and you'll see that these three sections are fairly equal in size. So if you need to find a certain word, start looking in the appropriate section.

A. Directions: Circle the word that correctly completes each sentence.

1. The word (*dogmatic / mentor*) is in the second section of the dictionary.

2. The word vindicate is defined in the (*second / third*) section.

3. If you wanted to look up benevolent, you would turn to the (*first / second*) section.

4. The word (*prominent / erudite*) can be found in the first section of the dictionary.

B. Directions: You know that words defined in the dictionary *(entry words)* are listed in alphabetical order. Practice your dictionary skills by listing the following words in alphabetical order.

lapel	adjourn	demerit	sentiment	romance	oblong	fragile
geology	cyclone	inquiry	yonder	ballast	genial	matrimony
erupt	heifer	lavish	zenith	wary	jazz	kidnap

1. _____   8. _____   15. _____
2. _____   9. _____   16. _____
3. _____   10. _____   17. _____
4. _____   11. _____   18. _____
5. _____   12. _____   19. _____
6. _____   13. _____   20. _____
7. _____   14. _____   21. _____

NAME _____ DATE _____

USING THE DICTIONARY 2

Developing dictionary skills is an important step toward building an adult vocabulary.

Notice the guide words at the top of each regular page in the dictionary. The guide word on the left is the first entry on the page. The word on the right is the last entry.

A | materialize　　　　　　　maudlin

B | dash　　　　　　　　　　dawdle

A. Directions: Cross out the words that would *not* be defined on page A (as shown above). Then use your imagination—or check a dictionary—to list three words that *would* appear on that page.

1. *maternal　　mayfly　　mattress　　material　　mature　　maze*

2. _____, _____, _____

B. Directions: Look at the guide words at the top of page B. Then circle the word or words that correctly complete(s) each sentence below.

1. Words that alphabetically fall (between / outside) the guide words will appear on that page.

2. If you're looking for the word *deactivate*, you will have to turn (back / forward) a page or two.

3. You (will / will not) find the word *daughter* on page B.

4. You can probably find the word *dart* on the page just (before / after) page B.

C. Directions: Circle the words that would appear on each page shown below.

gearing	generation
geezer	generous
gable	geode
general	gelatin
genius	gazebo

pliers	plump
pledge	plummet
poach	plow
plowshare	plaza
ploy	plywood

CCSS: L.7.4c, L.7.4d　　5

NAME _____   DATE _____

INFORMATION IN A DICTIONARY ENTRY 1

In a dictionary, the definition of a word is only one *part of the word's details.*

A dictionary entry lists inflected forms of the entry word. These forms include . . .

PLURALS	**VERB TENSES**	**COMPARATIVES AND SUPERLATIVES**
child / children	see / saw / seeing	easy / easier / easiest
life / lives	lie / lay / lying	bad / worse / worst

A. Directions: Check a dictionary if you need help spelling the *plural* of each word below.

1. **agony** _____
2. **tomato** _____
3. **father-in-law** _____
4. **mouse** _____
5. **thief** _____
6. **radius** _____

B. Directions: Check a dictionary if you need help completing the chart of *verb tenses*.

PRESENT TENSE	PAST TENSE	PARTICIPLE
1. _____ ➡	wrote ➡	writing
2. feed ➡	_____ ➡	feeding
3. go ➡	went ➡	_____
4. _____ ➡	sat ➡	sitting

C. Directions: A dictionary can help you identify the comparative and superlative forms of each entry word. Circle the word or words that correctly complete(s) each sentence.

1. The superlative form of *attractive* is (attractivest / most attractive).
2. The comparative form of *bored* is (border / more bored).
3. The superlative form of *few* is (fewer / fewest).
4. The comparative form of *colossal* is (more colossal / colossaler).

NAME _____ DATE _____

INFORMATION IN A DICTIONARY ENTRY 2

A. Directions: Some words have more than one acceptable spelling. Remember that the preferred spelling is always listed *first* in a dictionary entry. Complete the word pairs below with either the preferred spelling or its less common alternate.

1. _____ / omelette
2. octopuses / _____
3. _____ / larvas
4. _____ / teepee
5. leveled / _____
6. gladioluses / _____
7. _____ / make-up
8. hallelujah / _____

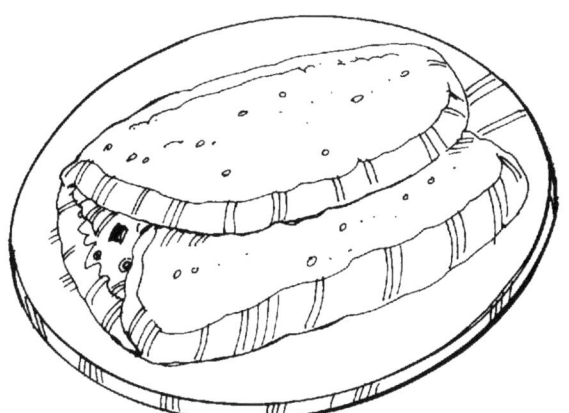

B. Directions: Some dictionaries include a word's *etymology*, or original source, before or after its definition. Draw a line to match each word with its origin.

1. **anemone**   a. from the Irish word *seamrog*, meaning "little clover"

2. **castanets**   b. named by Spanish dancers who saw that this instrument looked like two chestnuts

3. **catamaran**   c. from two Latin words, *unum* ("one") and *cornu* ("horn")

4. **geranium**   d. from the Tamil word *katta-marran*, meaning "tied wood"

5. **mercurial**   e. from two Greek words, *anemos* ("wind") and *mone* ("habitation")

6. **shamrock**   f. from *Mercury*, the fast messenger of the Roman gods

7. **unicorn**   g. named for the crane, *geranos* in Greek, because its seed pods look like a crane's head

NAME _____ DATE _____

DENOTATION AND CONNOTATION 1

A word's *denotation* is its literal meaning. The **connotation** *of the same word may be something quite different.*

A word's connotation is its implied meaning. Connotation arises from the ideas, emotions, and experiences associated with the word. Two words with nearly the same denotation may have very different connotations.

EXAMPLE:

opponent (positive connotation, suggesting a worthy competitor)

foe (negative connotation, suggesting an enemy)

A. Directions: Write **P** for *positive* or **N** for *negative* next to each word below.

1. _____ wretched
2. _____ unique
3. _____ survive
4. _____ gangster
5. _____ humane
6. _____ sneaky
7. _____ spry
8. _____ embarrass
9. _____ fantastic
10. _____ snob
11. _____ valiant
12. _____ wilt

B. Directions: Words in the box are *synonyms* (with different connotations) of the words below. Write the matching word from the box next to each word below. Hint: You will *not* use all the words.

| accumulate | custodian | devise | aroma | assertive | vigorous |
| bold | crowd | emphasize | doubtful | thin | persuade |

1. contrive / _____
2. aggressive / _____
3. mob / _____
4. hoard / _____
5. brainwash / _____
6. brazen / _____
7. janitor / _____
8. odor / _____
9. belabor / _____
10. gaunt / _____

8   CCSS: L.7.5, L.7.5b, L.7.5c

© Saddleback Educational Publishing • www.sdlback.com
Common Core Skills & Strategies for Vocabulary: Level 7

NAME _____   DATE _____

DENOTATION AND CONNOTATION 2

Making careful word choices ensures that you get your message across.

People use *euphemisms* to replace words that are thought to be too strong or unpleasant.
   EXAMPLE: *passed away* instead of *died*

Dysphemisms are harsher words deliberately used to replace neutral words.
   EXAMPLE: *quack* instead of *doctor*

Directions: Complete the chart below with the euphemisms, dysphemisms, or neutral words from the box on the right. Hint: You will *not* use all the words.

EUPHEMISM	NEUTRAL WORD	DYSPHEMISM
1. firm	obstinate	_____
2. fervent	_____	hysterical
3. _____	charity	handout
4. move on	leave	_____
5. assist	_____	abet
6. _____	unusual	abnormal
7. developing country	underdeveloped country	_____
8. challenged	_____	crippled
9. _____	worker	hireling
10. peacekeeper	_____	mercenary
11. man's best friend	dog	_____
12. _____	house	shack
13. lounge	_____	toilet

WORD LIST

abandon
abrupt
cur
diner
disabled
donation
emotional
employee
hash-house
help
mansion
pig-headed
quick
restaurant
restroom
rude
soldier
special
third-world

NAME _____ DATE _____

JUST FOR FUN: DICTIONARY CHALLENGE 1

Here's a chance to have some fun with some interesting and unusual words.

Directions: To answer the questions, study the dictionary definitions of the **boldface** words.

1. Would you use the word **redolent** or **refulgent** to describe a **pelargonium**? Explain your answer.
   _____
   _____
   _____

2. In what countries would you find **Qishm** and **Qiqihar**?
   _____
   _____

3. Would you rather have a voice that's **mellifluous** or **cacophonous**? Why?
   _____
   _____

4. Would you go to a **boutique** to buy some **borscht**? Why or why not?
   _____
   _____

5. Would the words **precursors**, **originators**, and **forebears** be used to describe your **progenitors** or your **progeny**? Explain your answer.
   _____
   _____

6. Who would make a better dinner companion—a **gourmand** or an **epicure**? Why?
   _____
   _____

7. Suppose you were in danger. Would you rather have someone **ameliorate** your situation or **exacerbate** it?
   _____
   _____

10 CCSS: L.7.4, L.7.4c, L.7.6

© Saddleback Educational Publishing • www.sdlback.com
Common Core Skills & Strategies for Vocabulary: Level 7

NAME _____ DATE _____

JUST FOR FUN: DICTIONARY CHALLENGE 2

Directions: To answer the questions, look up the dictionary definitions of the **boldface** words.

1. Would someone deliver a **eulogy** for a **euglena**? Explain why or why not.

   _____
   _____
   _____

2. What do a **hammada**, a **veldt**, and a **steppe** have in common?

   _____
   _____
   _____

3. In which country would you be likely to find **dolmades** at an **agora**?

   _____
   _____

4. What are some similarities and some differences between a **coati** and an **agouti**?

   _____
   _____

5. Would you rather babysit a child who was **obstreperous** or one who was **amiable**? Why?

   _____
   _____

6. When might you give an **octogenarian** a **cymbidium**? Explain your answer.

   _____
   _____

7. If you were a **tyro**, would you attempt to play a piano duet with a **virtuoso**? Why or why not?

   _____
   _____

NAME _____ DATE _____

PRONUNCIATION: VOWEL SOUNDS 1

Impressive use of language requires correct pronunciation.

Directions: Did you know that each vowel can stand for several different sounds? Which words have the same vowel sound as the **boldface** example word in parentheses? Circle two words in each group.

A SOUNDS

1. **short A (hat)**
   back   make
   began   space

2. **long A (day)**
   basic   volcano
   talk   audience

3. **AL (fall)**
   aim   jail
   almost falter

4. **AR (dare)**
   beware straw
   square start

5. **AR (jar)**
   careful hard
   party   parent

6. **schwa A (alone)**
   scald   laid
   another agree

E SOUNDS

1. **short E (end)**
   empty   being
   spell   legal

2. **long E (she)**
   secret elf
   female men

3. **silent e (place)**
   ever   something
   operate safety

4. **ER (her)**
   reflect baker
   camera brief

5. **schwa E (the)**
   happen item
   weapon fine

I SOUNDS

1. **short I (miss)**
   insect dinosaur
   idle   which

2. **long I (rice)**
   jingle wire
   whir   describe

3. **IR (stir)**
   dirty   shirt
   time   rinse

O SOUNDS

1. **short O (not)**
   opera   zero
   problem odor

2. **long O (ago)**
   got   ocean
   cargo   job

3. **OU / OW (out, cow)**
   young   sound
   crow   eyebrow

4. **OI / OY (spoil, boy)**
   voice   period
   joyous youth

5. **broad O (cross)**
   song   tooth
   wood   office

6. **short OO (book)**
   mood   cookie
   wooden zoo

7. **long OO (too)**
   stood   troop
   foot   bamboo

8. **schwa O (riot)**
   joint   canyon
   doily   method

12   CCSS: RF.5.3, RF.5.3a, L.7.2, L.7.4a, L.7.4c

NAME _____ DATE _____

PRONUNCIATION: VOWEL SOUNDS 2

A. Directions: Which words have the same vowel sound as the **boldface** example word in parentheses? Circle two words in each group.

U SOUNDS

1. short U (**sun**)   funny   museum   Utah   summer

2. long U (**use**)   January   jump   human   umpire

3. 1-dot U̇ (**full**)   tuna   bullfrog   murmur   cushion

4. 2-dot Ü (**flute**)   fur   prune   cruel   bully

5. UR (**curl**)   crude   nutrition   turtle   surface

B. Directions: Circle the word that correctly completes each sentence. Check the dictionary if you're not sure.

1. The word *stare* rhymes with (*there* / *here*).

2. The word *high* rhymes with (*aweigh* / *pie*).

3. The word *blown* rhymes with (*flown* / *crown*).

4. The word *measure* rhymes with (*reassure* / *treasure*).

5. They word *greed* rhymes with (*plead* / *dread*).

6. The word *billow* rhymes with (*allow* / *pillow*).

7. The word *about* rhymes with (*fraught* / *sauerkraut*).

8. The word *stood* rhymes with (*hood* / *mood*).

9. The word *aloud* rhymes with (*stowed* / *plowed*).

10. The word *tough* rhymes with (*enough* / *although*).

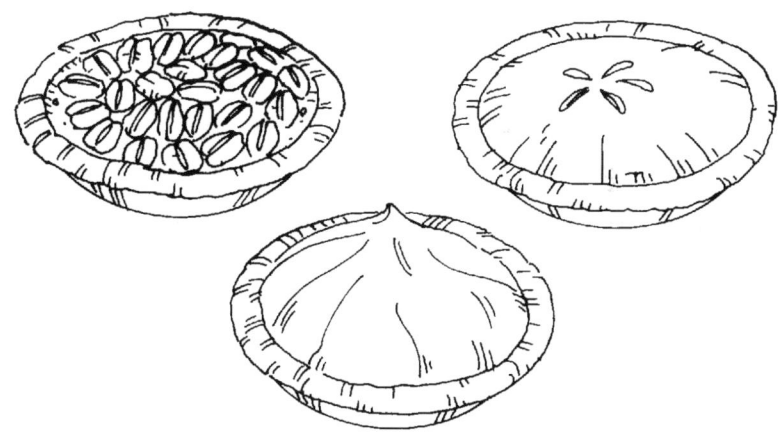

NAME _____   DATE _____

PRONUNCIATION: SILENT LETTERS 1

Remember that many English words have silent letters. If you're not sure how to pronounce a word, a dictionary can help you.

A. Directions: Say each word aloud. Use a dictionary if necessary. Then cross out two words in each group that do *not* have silent letters. Finally, write the silent letter you see in the other two words. The first one has been done for you.

SILENT LETTER

1. __c__ ~~inspect~~ scenic ~~color~~ ascend
2. _____ scheduling showing happy honest
3. _____ blow wander wilt wrap
4. _____ water fetch often patted
5. _____ could flap talk tassel
6. _____ gather align sugar gnu
7. _____ buzz numb amber thumb
8. _____ knot broken knitting mark
9. _____ psychology perhaps pseudonym important

B. Directions: Think of a word with a silent letter that answers each question. Write it on the line.

1. What dark color has a silent consonant? _____

2. Name a major organ in your body that has a silent letter. _____

3. Name a school subject that has a silent letter. _____

4. What numbers between one and ten have a silent letter or letters?
   _____

5. What's another word for *climb down*, *sink*, or *slip*? _____

NAME _____ DATE _____

PRONUNCIATION: SILENT LETTERS 2

A. Directions: To complete the sentences, unscramble the words containing silent letters. Use context clues for help.

1. The **(FEBTUF)** _____ lunch included soup, salad, and dessert.

2. We played a game of **(ROCUEQT)** _____ on the lawn.

3. The soldiers were all wearing **(AKHIK)** _____ uniforms.

4. During the holiday season, we always hang **(LITEMOSTE)** _____ over our door.

5. This lingering cold makes me feel just **(CEWETHRD)** _____!

6. The large family rented **(JONANIDIG)** _____ rooms at the hotel.

B. Directions: Use the clues and the first letters to help you solve the crossword puzzle. Answers are words containing the silent letters shown in parentheses.

ACROSS

1. **(G, H)** one of the five senses
4. **(H)** truthful
5. **(T)** an amount of cookie dough
9. **(B)** one who owes money

DOWN

2. **(G, H)** a part of the body
3. **(G)** the time for which a king rules
5. **(T, E)** a hair of a hog, used for brushes
6. **(D, E)** container for printer ink
7. **(C)** shiny varnish
8. **(D)** a little person

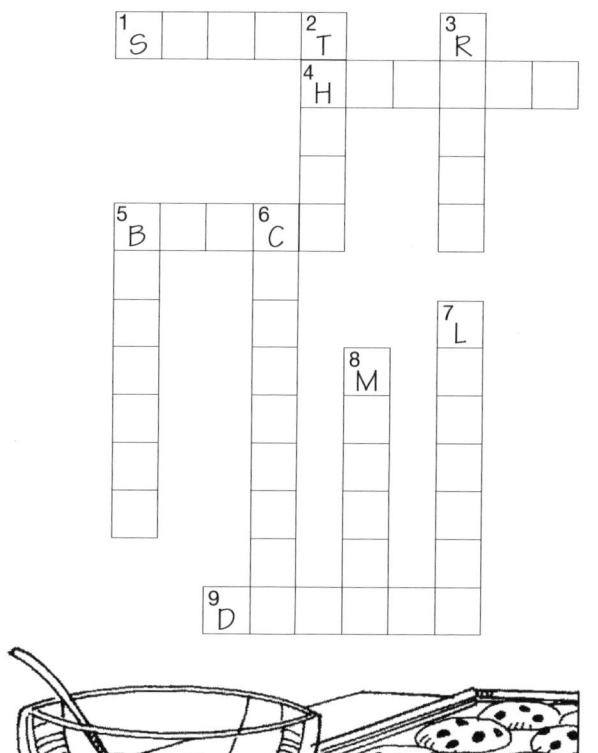

NAME _____ DATE _____

PRONUNCIATION: SYLLABLES AND ACCENT MARKS 1

A word's syllables are its separate sounds. The word kitten, *for example, has two syllables:* kit *and* ten. *Some words, like* cat, *have only one syllable. Syllable breaks can help you pronounce long words, one sound at a time.*

A. Directions: Count the syllables in each word in the box. Then check a dictionary to make sure you separated the sounds correctly. Finally, copy the divided words under the correct heading. Use centered dots to indicate syllable breaks. The first one has been done as an example.

doubtful	melancholy	developmental	oversight
disagreeable	orchid	continuous	comedy
blockade	geological	bungalow	considerate
tallow	acknowledge	affectionate	organization

1. **2-SYLLABLE WORDS**
   doubt•ful
   _____
   _____
   _____

3. **4-SYLLABLE WORDS**
   _____
   _____
   _____
   _____

2. **3-SYLLABLE WORDS**
   _____
   _____
   _____
   _____

4. **5-SYLLABLE WORDS**
   _____
   _____
   _____
   _____

When you checked the boxed words in the dictionary, did you notice the accent mark (´) placed somewhere in each word? It shows which syllable is **stressed** in pronunciation. Think about the word trophy (tro´• phy), for example. The accent shows that the emphasis is on the first syllable—tro. This tells you that the pronunciation is TROphy, not troPHY.

B. Directions: Use capital letters, as in TROphy, to show the correct pronunciation of the following words.

1. atlas _____
2. phenomenon _____
3. complicate _____
4. irregular _____

NAME _____ DATE _____

PRONUNCIATION: SYLLABLES AND ACCENT MARKS 2

A. Directions: As you read the sentences, say the **boldface** words aloud. Then circle the word that correctly completes the second sentence.

1. If you throw a **boomerang** correctly, it will come back to you.

   The (first / second / third) syllable is accented.

2. Carmen puts just enough **cinnamon** in her pumpkin pie filling.

   The (first / second / third) syllable is accented.

3. Jackie's father plays first violin in our city's **symphony** orchestra.

   The (first / second / third) syllable is accented.

4. This **publication** comes out the first week of every month.

   The (first / second / third) syllable is accented.

5. That **ferocious** dog is a danger to everyone in the neighborhood.

   The (second / third / fourth) syllable is accented.

6. The **horizontal** stripes on my bedroom wallpaper are yellow.

   The (second / third / fourth) syllable is accented.

7. Patrick and his friends **participate** in after-school baseball.

   The (first / second / third) syllable is accented.

8. The policeman ordered the suspect to **reveal** the name of his accomplice.

   The (first / second) syllable is accented.

B. Directions: Place the accent marks in these words. Check a dictionary if you're not sure where they go.

1. contest (noun)	con • test	3. **replay** (noun)	re • play
contest (verb)	con • test	**replay** (verb)	re • play
2. conduct (verb)	con • duct	4. **address** (verb)	ad • dress
conduct (noun)	con • duct	**address** (noun)	ad • dress

NAME _____ DATE _____

USING CONTEXT CLUES 1

If you don't know a word's meaning, you can often make a good guess by studying the other words in the sentence.

Directions: First, circle the nonsense word in each sentence. Then use context clues to help you decide what the word probably means. Finally, circle a letter to show the word's meaning.

1. He was such a good skier we couldn't believe that he was a jimple.

   a. beginner   b. man   c. New Yorker

2. Because I get sunburned so easily, I always avoid going to the dipdop.

   a. kitchen   b. car   c. beach

3. We grew too many tomatoes, so we gave the krinskis to the neighbors.

   a. leaves   b. extras   c. zucchini

4. Our teacher sloozed us for being rude to the guest.

   a. criticized   b. praised   c. thanked

5. A promise of "something for nothing" is usually a schlimper.

   a. guarantee   b. fraud   c. coupon

6. Joe's gairblue over his dog's death continued for many months.

   a. gratitude   b. joy   c. grief

7. To remain on the team, you must flang the coach's rules.

   a. follow   b. break   c. disrespect

8. If our best player is moglump, our chances of winning will not be good.

   a. strong   b. active   c. ill

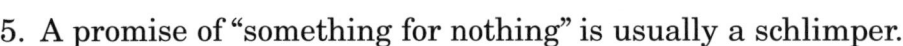

NAME _____ DATE _____

USING CONTEXT CLUES 2

If you come across an unfamiliar word and don't have a dictionary handy, use these four strategies:

- *the general sense of the sentence or passage (combined with your prior knowledge)*
- *synonyms or restated definitions of the unfamiliar word*
- *examples of the unfamiliar word given in the passage*
- *familiar words or ideas used to compare or contrast with the unfamiliar word*

Directions: Use the strategies listed above to help you guess the meaning of the nonsense word in each sentence. Circle a letter to show your answer.

1. The elephant in the circus parade looked **lodsjiled** to the small boy.
   a. enormous
   b. lopsided
   c. tiny

2. The orator's **onevul** speech made half the audience fall asleep.
   a. wonderful
   b. boring
   c. exciting

3. After Grace's **bindu** welcome, all of her guests felt right at home.
   a. rude
   b. half-hearted
   c. warm

4. After our long hike on the steep trail, we all suffered from **fepsduf**.
   a. anger
   b. worry
   c. fatigue

5. Because of the fire danger, the fire department **matoxes** the use of candles in this theater.
   a. forbids
   b. approves
   c. encourages

6. The gently falling snow **incobbled** like diamonds in the moonlight.
   a. melted
   b. sold
   c. glistened

NAME _____ DATE _____

NOUNS: GETTING MEANING FROM CONTEXT CLUES

You already know that a noun names a person (boy, Steven), a place (city, Los Angeles), or a thing (sport, football). All the answers in this exercise are nouns.

Directions: Read each incomplete sentence. Then use the **boldface** word or words to help you figure out the scrambled word. Write it on the line.

1. I had a strong **urge** to buy a new dress, but I resisted the **(PILMUSE)** _____.

2. Henry's **truthfulness** earned him a reputation for **(THESONY)** _____.

3. After the **team** played so well, the coach praised the **(YESLARP)** _____ for their hard work.

4. His **quest** for the treasure was a **(RECSHA)** _____ that took 10 years.

5. The **movie** had such an abrupt ending that I thought the **(IMFL)** _____ had broken.

6. His **(TAMPETT)** _____ to fix the leaky pipe was an **effort** that ended in failure.

7. After two years without **precipitation**, last night's **(LAILFRAN)** _____ was very welcome.

8. We beat the team that had been in third **place**, so our **(NIPSIOTO)** _____ changed.

20   CCSS: L.7.1, L.7.4a, L.7.4c, L.7.2b

© Saddleback Educational Publishing • www.sdlback.com
Common Core Skills & Strategies for Vocabulary: Level 7

NAME _____ DATE _____

VERBS: GETTING MEANING FROM CONTEXT CLUES

This exercise tests your **verbal skills.** *Remember that a* **verb** *is a word that expresses an* **action** *(He jumped.) or a* **state of being** *(She is a good student.).*

Directions: Read the incomplete sentences. Then use the **boldface** words as clues to help you figure out the scrambled words.

1. I can **handle** the hand lawn mower, but I don't know how to **(RETEPAO)** _____ the electric one.

2. The wish to succeed that **compels** you to study hard **(ROFECS)** _____ me to keep up with you.

3. If you **grumble** and **(MACINLOP)** _____ about the homework, you'll annoy the teacher.

4. We **compared** and **(TACDROTENS)** _____ the two houses before deciding which one to buy.

5. After Caesar's army **beat** one country, they soon **(QUEDCORNE)** _____ another.

6. Not only did Brendon **hurt** his arm, he also **(JIRNUDE)** _____ his knee.

7. Melissa's ability to **sing and dance** helped her **(REFPORM)** _____ well on stage.

8. First she felt **weak and dizzy**, and then she **(NATFIDE)** _____ .

9. Don't let unworthy goals **attract** you and **(MTTEP)** _____ you to do foolish things.

10. You will **ruin** that shirt if you **(ROCSHC)** _____ it with a hot iron.

© Saddleback Educational Publishing • www.sdlback.com
Common Core Skills & Strategies for Vocabulary: Level 7
CCSS: L.7.1, L.7.4a, L.7.4c, L.7.2b   21

NAME _____ DATE _____

ADJECTIVES: GETTING MEANING FROM CONTEXT CLUES

Adjectives *describe nouns or pronouns by answering such questions as* **how many?** *(ten years) or* **what kind?** *(leather jacket). Adjectives can make your communication colorful and interesting.*

Directions: Read the incomplete sentences. Then use the **boldface** words as clues to help you figure out the scrambled word. Write it on the line.

1. We love our mountain cabin because it is so **calm** and **(CEFPUELA)** _____ there.

2. When the **poor** man was robbed, he became **(TEUDITSTE)** _____.

3. Hiding in the dark, my friends were so quiet their sudden shout of "Surprise!" left me **(CESSHEPELS)** _____ .

4. **Shy** Melissa was so **(SHUBFAL)** _____ that she couldn't speak in front of the class.

5. Yesterday was especially **busy**, or **(THECIC)** _____, because Uncle Dan came to visit and the cat had kittens on the couch.

6. The **tough** meat was very **(FIDCUFLIT)** _____ to chew.

7. The **hard** mattress was too **(MIRF)** _____ to be really comfortable.

8. I feel sure of an **easy** A on that **(MILSEP)** _____ math test.

9. The **(HELMUB)** _____ home was decorated in a **plain** style.

10. Our **stroll** in the park filled up our **(SILUELREY)** _____ afternoon.

22   CCSS: L.7.1, L.7.4a, L.7.4c, L.7.2b

© Saddleback Educational Publishing • www.sdlback.com
Common Core Skills & Strategies for Vocabulary: Level 7

NAME _____ DATE _____

ADVERBS: GETTING MEANING FROM CONTEXT CLUES

Adverbs *answer such questions as* **when?** *(arrived* later*),* **how?** *(spoke* timidly*),* **where?** *(put it* there*),* **how often?** *(danced* daily*), and* **to what extent?** *(*completely *satisfied).*

Directions: Complete each sentence with the most appropriate adverb. Use the **boldface** words as clues. Check a dictionary if you need help with word meaning.

1. It's just a **guess**, but I think there are _____ 15 minutes left on the parking meter. (exactly / approximately / never)

2. After his mother told him to share, the **selfish** little boy _____ offered his playmate one of his toys. (generously / happily / reluctantly)

3. Wanting a **clean** and allergy-proof room, Theresa _____ vacuumed the carpets. (thoroughly / barely / hastily)

4. The **warm**, friendly host _____ welcomed his guests. (shyly / cordially / fearfully)

5. The teacher _____ known as Miss Cooper is **now** called Mrs. Washington. (actually / sadly / formerly)

6. **Basically** and _____, Christopher believes in the value of charity. (fundamentally / shakily / shallowly)

7. Right now I can repay you only _____, but I'll get the **rest** to you soon. (totally / immediately / partially)

8. The hurricane tore _____ through the town, **destroying** all the homes in its path. (peacefully / violently / quietly)

9. "I will _____ sign that confession," said the prisoner, "because I am **innocent**!" (gladly / soon / never)

10. The **perpetual** flame has been burning _____ since John F. Kennedy was buried here. (continuously / intermittently / weakly)

NAME _____ DATE _____

FORMS OF A WORD: ADJECTIVE TO NOUN 1

Adjectives *(words that describe)* can usually be rewritten as nouns *(beautiful ‹ beauty)*. Remember to keep a dictionary handy to check your spelling.

A. Directions: Notice that all clues are adjectives. Complete the crossword puzzle with the noun form of each adjective.

ACROSS

4. creative
5. brutal
6. glandular
7. solitary

DOWN

1. accurate
2. hostile
3. prestigious
4. changeable

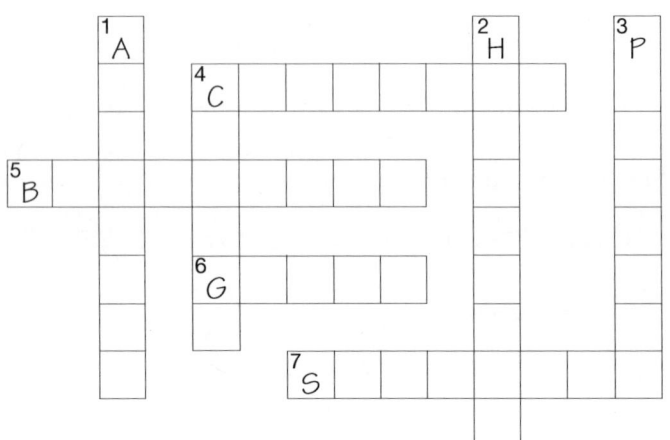

B. Directions: Now use one of the puzzle answer words to complete each sentence below.

1. Because her thyroid _____ doesn't work properly, Ana's metabolism has slowed down.

2. Have you noticed the recent _____ in that child's behavior?

3. Hector is so proud of his _____ that he's entering it in the art contest.

4. Jeremy needs at least one hour of _____ each day for meditation.

5. Myra's good job gives her _____ in the community.

6. I reported the unkind pet owner's _____ to the police.

7. The mistreated animal exhibited _____ toward his owner.

8. When you measure ingredients for baking, _____ is very important.

NAME _____ DATE _____

FORMS OF A WORD: ADJECTIVE TO NOUN 2

Directions: Read the phrases. Then write the noun form of each **boldface** adjective. Finally, write an original sentence using that noun.

1. **affectionate** gesture _____
   _____
   _____
   _____
   _____

2. **considerate** behavior _____
   _____

3. **eternal** love _____
   _____

4. **fearless** warrior _____
   _____

5. **venomous** poison _____
   _____

6. **turbulent** winds _____
   _____

7. **suspicious** activity _____
   _____

8. **sentimental** journey _____
   _____

9. **residential** neighborhood _____
   _____

10. **punctual** arrival _____
    _____

11. **monotonous** speech _____
    _____

NAME _____   DATE _____

FORMS OF A WORD: VERB TO ADJECTIVE 1

It isn't difficult to rewrite verbs as adjectives (enjoy ‹ enjoyable). Remember to keep a dictionary nearby to check your spelling.

A. Directions: Notice that all clue words can be used as *verbs*. Complete the crossword puzzle with the *adjective* form of each verb.

ACROSS
2. prefer
4. filter
6. punctuate
8. dry

DOWN
1. warrant
3. dimple
5. die
7. tie

B. Directions: Write an answer word from the puzzle next to the definition it matches.

1. _____ : no longer living
2. _____ : more desirable
3. _____ : having a small hollow on the cheek or chin
4. _____ : describing water or other fluid that has had its impurities removed
5. _____ : describing something that has had all the water removed
6. _____ : said or done with special force

C. Directions: Write sentences using the adjective form of each verb listed.

1. *believe* _____
2. *enjoy* _____
3. *prefer* _____

NAME _____ DATE _____

FORMS OF A WORD: VERB TO ADJECTIVE 2

Directions: First write the *adjective* form of each **boldface** word. Then write an original sentence using that adjective.

1. to **sustain** a note _____
   _____
   _____
   _____

2. to **warp** a piece of wood _____
   _____

3. to **reject** a plan _____
   _____

4. to **radiate** light _____
   _____

5. to **rebel** against an oppressor _____
   _____

6. to **recognize** a friend _____
   _____

7. to **excel** in a sport _____
   _____

8. to **succeed** in a job _____
   _____

9. to **modify** a recipe _____
   _____

10. to **persist** in a task _____
    _____

11. to **intend** to get organized _____
    _____

NAME _____ DATE _____

FORMS OF A WORD: NOUN TO VERB 1

How do you rewrite a noun as a verb? Example: **competition ‹ compete.** *Some of these changes can be tricky, so keep a dictionary handy.*

A. Directions: Notice that the **boldface** clues are *nouns* (naming words). Puzzle answers are the *verb* form of each noun. Check a dictionary if you need help.

ACROSS

3. a careful **consumer**
4. window **draperies**
5. a lucky **rescue**
6. a feeling of **hatred**

DOWN

1. an exciting **drama**
2. a young **dependent**
3. a difficult **complication**

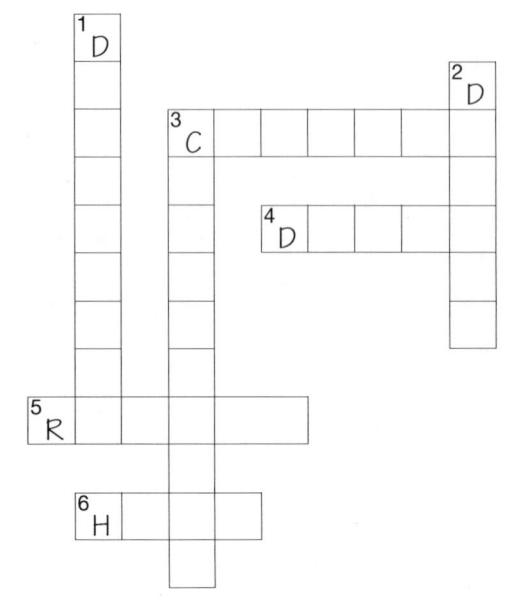

B. Directions: Now use one of the puzzle answer words to complete each sentence below.

1. The lifeguard will _____ the desperate swimmer.

2. I absolutely _____ the smell of skunks.

3. Our large family can _____ two loaves of bread a day.

4. Sheryl and Joe seem to _____ every unimportant little event.

5. Those lazy teenagers _____ on their parents for everything.

6. This new requirement will _____ our task considerably.

7. We can _____ the fabric gracefully around the display.

NAME _____ DATE _____

FORMS OF A WORD: NOUN TO VERB 2

Directions: First write the *verb* form of each **boldface** noun. Then write an original sentence using that verb.

1. another **postponement** _____
   _____

2. engine **lubrication** _____
   _____

3. **conviction** of the suspect _____
   _____

4. an uncomfortable **confrontation** _____
   _____

5. regular **correspondence** _____
   _____

6. a surprising **development** _____
   _____

7. military **organization** _____
   _____

8. shallow **penetration** _____
   _____

9. total **paralysis** _____
   _____

10. an interesting **narrative** _____
    _____

11. accurate **representation** _____
    _____

NAME _____ DATE _____

JUST FOR FUN: WORD LADDERS 1

Word play makes vocabulary-building more fun. Have some fun discovering how much difference a letter or two can make.

A. Directions: Change one letter in each **boldface** word to complete the word ladder. Use the clues to help you figure out the words. As an example, the first one has been done for you.

1. **RAKE**
   - _bake_ do to bread
   - _lake_ body of water
   - _cake_ birthday treat

2. **CARE**
   - _____ without clothing
   - _____ a bold move
   - _____ big bunny

3. **TIDE**
   - _____ travel by car
   - _____ a square has four
   - _____ opposite of seek

4. **ZEST**
   - _____ a bother
   - _____ exam
   - _____ good, better

5. **WEAK**
   - _____ a bird has one
   - _____ drip from a faucet
   - _____ type of wood

6. **TOOT**
   - _____ type of shoe
   - _____ a plant has one
   - _____ pirate treasure

B. Directions: Now change *two* letters in each word to complete the following word ladders.

1. **QUACK**
   - _____ for a train
   - _____ a pile
   - _____ a dark color

2. **SHEEP**
   - _____ another word for crawl
   - _____ take a nap
   - _____ a baby bird's sound

3. **SPILL**
   - _____ to make cold
   - _____ motionless
   - _____ to barbecue

4. **STAKE**
   - _____ to stop a car
   - _____ a piece of snow
   - _____ a male duck

NAME _____ DATE _____

JUST FOR FUN: WORD LADDERS 2

A. Directions: Make new words by adding one letter at the *beginning* of each short word. The first one has been done for you.

1. _s_ talk
   _s_ pin
   _s_ age

2. ___lash
   ___lag
   ___act

3. ___rain
   ___lob
   ___old

4. ___ale
   ___ant
   ___arch

5. ___art
   ___ore
   ___reek

6. ___one
   ___ail
   ___either

B. Directions: This time you will make new words by adding one letter at the *end* of each short word.

1. plan___
   for___
   car___

2. pan___
   tan___
   ban___

3. for___
   nor___
   war___

4. tar___
   see___
   dam___

C. Directions: Now add a letter somewhere *inside* the short word to make a new word. The first one has been done for you.

1. cap _clap, camp, chap, or carp_
2. fame _____
3. base _____
4. bag _____
5. cot _____
6. hug _____
7. pose _____
8. lie _____

NAME _____ DATE _____

MAKING COMPOUND WORDS 1

Some words are made up of two smaller words. **Sunflower** *and* **airline** *are examples of familiar* **compound** *words.*

A. Directions:

Combine words from the first list with words from the second list to make compound words. Write a letter to show which words go together. The first one has been done for you.

1. _j_ hair _cut_____ a. crow
2. ____ wrist_____ b. back
3. ____ air_____ c. watch
4. ____ out_____ d. fall
5. ____ scare_____ e. port
6. ____ touch_____ f. ware
7. ____ water_____ g. bite
8. ____ over_____ h. cake
9. ____ pan_____ i. side
10. ____ sky_____ j. cut
11. ____ silver_____ k. fast
12. ____ paper_____ l. down
13. ____ break_____ m. scraper

B. Directions:

In the squares below, draw pictures to illustrate three of the compound words you made. Write the word under each picture.

WORD: _____

WORD: _____

WORD: _____

32   CCSS: L.7.4, L.7.4a, L.7.3, L.7.5

Common Core Skills & Strategies for Vocabulary: Level 7

NAME _____ DATE _____

MAKING COMPOUND WORDS 2

A. Directions: Use vowels (a, e, i, o, u) to complete the compound words.

1. A ballerina sometimes dances on her t_pt___s.

2. Mom said to put the clean dishes in the c_pb___rd.

3. Did you ever make tea from p_pp_rm_nt leaves?

4. The sp_tl_ght was on the star of the play as she sang her solo.

5. The baby sits in the h_ghch___r to eat her meals.

6. Lester likes to wear a sw__tsh_rt featuring his school's logo.

7. There's a w_ndm_ll in the park's tulip garden.

B. Directions: Solve the crossword puzzle with familiar compound words. Use the clues for help.

ACROSS

1. a mental image of a scene from the past
4. combination of clothes that go together
6. a long braid of hair
7. use this to wash dishes

DOWN

2. person in charge at the beach
3. one way to get to school
5. a pet in a bowl of water
6. mail sent from your vacation

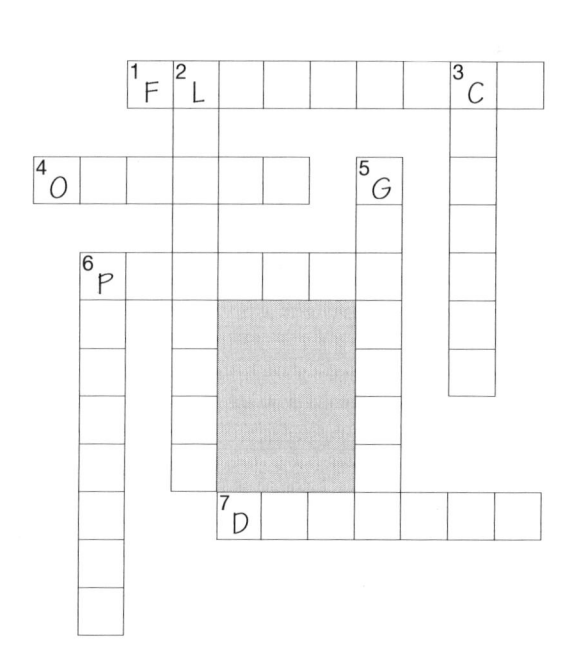

NAME _____ DATE _____

COMPOUND WORDS: *HEAD* AND *FOOT* 1

These questions will help you show off what you know about compound words.

A. Directions: First write *head* or *foot* to complete each compound word. Then draw a line to match each word with its meaning.

1. _____ phone   a. mark left in wet sand
2. _____ bridge   b. big print in a newspaper
3. _____ note   c. piece of furniture that goes with a chair
4. _____ lights   d. device for listening to music privately
5. _____ print   e. construction that goes over a river
6. _____ stool   f. information at the bottom of a page
7. _____ line   g. lamps in the front of a car (or lights on a stage)

B. Directions: Use words from the box to complete the answer words. Then solve the crossword puzzle.

| ache | ball | band | board | hunter | locker | quarters |

ACROSS

2. The corporate _head_ found a good employee for the position.
5. _Foot_ can be a very violent sport.
6. Carol uses a _head_ to keep the hair out of her eyes.

DOWN

1. Marge has a painful _head_.
3. His company's _head_ is located in Chicago.
4. The _foot_ of the bed is handcarved.
5. The soldier's _foot_ was kept very neat.

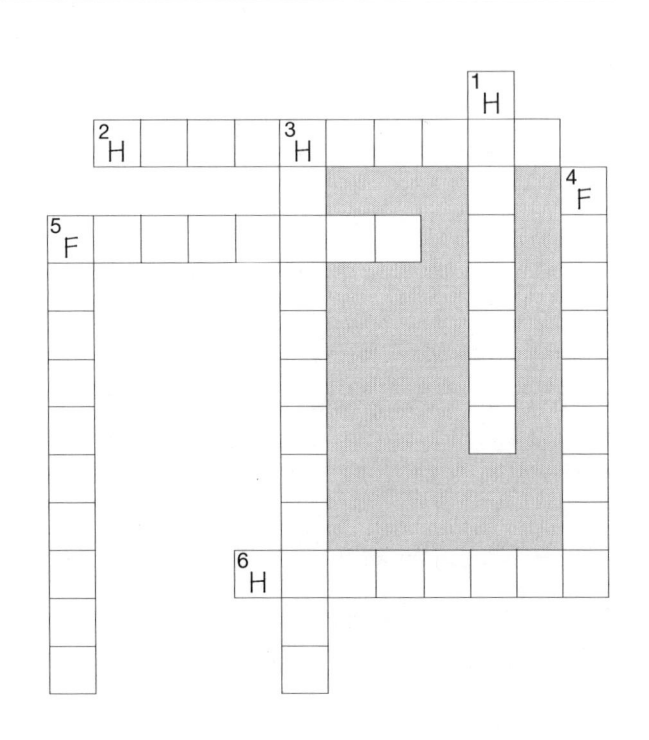

34   CCSS: L.7.4, L.7.4a, L.7.3, L.7.5

NAME _____ DATE _____

COMPOUND WORDS: *HEAD* AND *FOOT* 2

Directions: Use the context clues to help you figure out the incomplete compound words. Check a dictionary if you need help.

1. Some Native Americans used to wear beautiful *head*_____ made of feathers.

2. A mountain climber must get a good *foot*_____ as he climbs.

3. The fancy *head*_____ of that bed is made of solid maple.

4. Burt came hurtling down the waterslide *head*_____.

5. The *foot*_____ carried by her shop includes shoes, boots, and sandals.

6. The telephone operator wore a *head*_____ to keep her hands free.

7. Wanda could hear heavy *foot*_____ coming up the stairs.

8. Kim likes to think of herself as "*foot*_____ and fancy free."

9. We made good *head*_____ in spite of the strong wind.

10. The senior citizens enjoyed walking on the *foot*_____ by the river.

11. Sixteen runners competed in the *foot*_____ through the woods.

12. The wrestler held his opponent in a mighty *head*_____.

NAME _____   DATE _____

COMPOUND WORDS: *AIR* AND *WATER* 1

A. Directions: Unscramble the words to complete the sentences. Hint: All the scrambled words begin with *air* or *water*.

1. Doris stores beans and rice in **(TIHATRIG)** _____ containers.

2. The tiny dragonfly stopped to rest on the **(TYLWILEAR)** _____.

3. An **(IRALIMA)** _____ letter takes two days to get here from Dallas.

4. A leak caused the boat to become **(GETDARLOWEG)** _____.

5. We got to the **(ROITARP)** _____ early to go through security.

6. Tom led us on a hike to see a spectacular **(TELWALFAR)** _____.

B. Directions: Use words from the box to complete the answer words. Then use the completed words to solve the puzzle.

| brush | colors | front | line | melon | sick | waves |

ACROSS

2. Radio signals travel over the _air_.

4. Which do you like better, _water_ or oil paintings?

5. Whenever she flies, Amy gets _air_.

6. We ate a big _water_ and kept the seeds for planting.

7. The _water_ on the ship is higher when the hold is heavy with cargo.

DOWN

1. The seafood restaurant is located on the _water_.

3. We used an _air_ to apply paint to the fence.

NAME _____ DATE _____

COMPOUND WORDS: *AIR* AND *WATER* 2

Directions: Use context clues to help you figure out the compound words beginning with *air* and *water*. Check a dictionary if you need more ideas.

1. Ducks, geese, and swans are different kinds of *water*_____.

2. Good-quality paper often has a *water*_____, a design produced by pressure during manufacture.

3. Tests proved that the helicopter was *air*_____, or safe for flying.

4. This vinyl raincoat is guaranteed to be *water*_____.

5. The fighter jets began an *air*_____ on the city.

6. The cook added *water*_____, an edible plant related to the nasturtium, to our sandwiches.

7. That hang glider has been *air*_____ for 30 minutes.

8. This will be little Alice's first flight in an *air*_____.

9. The flashlight was encased in a *water*_____ container.

10. That country does not allow military jets to fly in its *air*_____.

11. Niagara Falls is a very large and famous *water*_____.

NAME _____   DATE _____

COMPOUND WORDS: SUN AND WIND   1

A. Directions: First write *sun* or *wind* to complete each compound word. Then draw a line to match each word with its meaning.

1. _____ bag
2. _____ glasses
3. _____ sock
4. _____ down
5. _____ rise
6. _____ breaker
7. _____ dial

a. another word for sunset
b. another word for dawn
c. a lightweight jacket
d. a person who talks too much
e. a device that indicates time with shadows
f. fashion item that protects eyes
g. a cloth tube attached to the top of a pole that shows which way the wind is blowing

B. Directions: Use words from the box to complete the puzzle answers.

| burn | storms | surfed | shield | tan | roof | bonnet | fall |

ACROSS

1. *Wind* _____ can uproot even very big trees.
4. *Sun* _____ can inflame your skin and cause blisters.
6. Barry *wind* _____ on the bay.
7. Lydia got a great *sun* _____ in Hawaii.
8. We need new *wind* _____ wipers on our car.

DOWN

2. While gardening, Elizabeth wore a pink *sun* _____.
3. Sam's new car has a *sun* _____.
5. Tim's surprise inheritance was quite a *wind* _____.

38   CCSS: L.7.4, L.7.4a, L.7.3, L.7.5

© Saddleback Educational Publishing • www.sdlback.com
Common Core Skills & Strategies for Vocabulary: Level 7

NAME _____ DATE _____

COMPOUND WORDS: *SUN* AND *WIND* 2

Directions: Use context clues to help you figure out the compound words. If you need help completing the words, check a dictionary.

1. A *wind*_____ is a large sailing ship that is especially fast.

2. A beautiful *sun*_____ found its way through the thick trees and shone on the forest floor.

3. The *wind*_____ factor made the frigid air seem even colder.

4. Holland is famous for its great number of *wind*_____.

5. By sitting under a *sun*_____, you can get an even tan without going outside.

6. Henry choked when he got a piece of chicken caught in his *wind*_____.

7. Betty likes to *sun*_____ by lying in a hammock in her backyard.

8. Bluegill and black bass are types of *sun*_____, which swim in freshwater lakes and rivers.

9. Ellen likes the *wind*_____, casual look for her hair.

10. Annie puts *sun*_____ on her baby before taking him outdoors in the sun.

11. A *sun*_____ is a tall annual plant with big yellow blooms.

NAME _____ DATE _____

CHOOSING PRECISE WORDS 1

Choosing words with exact meanings greatly improves your communication skills.

A. Directions: Write **G** for *general* or **S** for *specific* to identify each word below. Then write a specific example for each general word or a word that names a general category for each specific word. The first two have been done for you.

1. _G_ dessert _ice cream_
2. _S_ autumn _season_
3. ____ animal _____
4. ____ diamond _____
5. ____ jewelry _____
6. ____ flower _____
7. ____ green _____
8. ____ salmon _____

B. Directions: Make 10 pairs of synonyms from the words in the box. Check a dictionary if you're not sure of word meanings. Then write the words under the proper headings. The first one has been done for you.

abhor	adore	apologize	admire	alone
absurd	atone	dislike	disagree	domination
entertain	ecstatic	enthrall	foolish	isolated
hobby	glad	obsession	influence	oppose

	MORE INTENSE	LESS INTENSE		MORE INTENSE	LESS INTENSE
1.	abhor	dislike	6.		
2.			7.		
3.			8.		
4.			9.		
5.			10.		

NAME _____   DATE _____

CHOOSING PRECISE WORDS 2

A thesaurus *is the best place to find synonyms*

Directions: First, unscramble the first specific synonym for each **boldface** general word. Then write original sentences using any two of the specific words. The first one has been done for you as an example.

GENERAL WORD	MORE SPECIFIC WORDS

1. **change** (RAVY) ___*vary*___, modify, evolve, grow, ripen, mellow, mature, transform
   a. *If the peaches are too hard, wait until they ripen.*
   b. *If your plans don't work out, modify them.*

2. **entertain** (SEAMU) _____, cheer, please, delight, divert, charm, captivate, stimulate
   a. _____
   b. _____

3. **interesting** (GANEGGNI) _____, pleasing, enchanting, satisfying, fascinating, absorbing
   a. _____
   b. _____

4. **answer** (SENDROP) _____, echo, react, rebut, argue, retort, remark
   a. _____
   b. _____

5. **run** (SNIRPT) _____, amble, gallop, canter, scamper, race, rush, dash
   a. _____
   b. _____

6. **sad** (MUGL) _____, sorrowful, downcast, gloomy, depressed, morose, grieved
   a. _____
   b. _____

NAME _____ DATE _____

GREEK ROOTS 1

If you know Greek roots, you can unlock the meaning of many English words.

ROOT	MEANING	EXAMPLE	ROOT	MEANING	EXAMPLE
cycl	circle, ring	bicycle, cyclone	dem	people	democracy, demogogue
gram	letter, written	telegram, diagram	gnos	know	agnostic, diagnostic
phon	sound	phonogram, telephone	lith	stone	lithograph, monolith
cardi	heart	cardiac, cardiogram	andr	man	androgynous, androphobia

Directions: Use the roots in the box above to complete the words in the sentences.

1. According to the doctor, Beth's p r o _ _ _ _ _ i s was good.

2. The t e l e _ _ _ _ with the shocking news arrived at midnight.

3. My mother's _ _ _ _ _ _ o l o g i s t is a highly respected heart doctor.

4. The toddler enjoyed her new red t r i _ _ _ _ e.

5. We enjoyed the s y m _ _ _ _ y at the new center for the arts.

6. This tool dates from the p a l e o _ _ _ _ _ i c age.

7. The AIDS e p i _ _ _ i c is especially devastating in Africa.

8. A woman who has two or more husbands at the same time is guilty of p o l y _ _ _ _ y.

9. A m i c r o _ _ _ _ e can help a speaker's voice carry to the back of the room.

10. The study of _ _ _ _ _ i c s helps children relate letters to their sounds.

11. The _ _ _ _ o p s has one large round eye in the center of his forehead.

12. Dad is a Republican, but Mom is a _ _ _ o c r a t.

42 CCSS: L.7.2b, L.7.4, L.7.4a, L.7.4b, L.7.6

NAME _____ DATE _____

GREEK ROOTS 2

You can often guess the meaning of a Greek root by thinking about the words in which it appears. For example: **archenemy, monarch.** *Perhaps the root* **arch** *means "chief."*

A. Directions: Notice the root in both example words. Then draw a line to connect each root with its meaning. Check a dictionary if you need help.

1. *dogma*tic, *dogma*tism   a. shape
2. *pod*iatrist, tri*pod*   b. love
3. *paleo*ntology, *paleo*lithic   c. foot
4. *neo*classic, *neo*phyte   d. opinion
5. meta*morph*osis, *morph*ology   e. old
6. *phil*osophy, *phil*anthropist f. new

B. Directions: Use the example words to help you guess the meaning of the root.

1. *opt*ician, *opt*ometrist   The root *opt* must mean _____.
2. claustro*phobia*, aqua*phobia*   The root *phobia* must mean _____.
3. *the*ology, a*the*ist   The root *the* must mean _____.

C. Directions: Read the root, its meaning, and the example word. Then add one more word that includes this root.

ROOT	MEANING	EXAMPLES
1. kine, cine	movement	*kinetic*, _____
2. lys	break down	*analysis*, _____
3. mania	madness	*pyromania*, _____
4. esth	feeling	*esthetic*, _____

NAME _____ DATE _____

LATIN ROOTS 1

Many English words contain Latin roots. The Latin roots in the chart will help to complete this exercise.

ROOT	MEANING	EXAMPLE	ROOT	MEANING	EXAMPLE
don	give	*donation*	cline	lean	*incline*
cur	care	*manicure*	cogn	know	*incognito*
cord	heart	*cordial*	man	hand	*manual*
mar	sea	*maritime*	ped	foot	*pedal*

Directions: Use the roots in the box to complete the words in the sentences.

1. The s u b _ _ _ _ _ _ _ was underwater for a week-long training exercise.

2. Darlene had changed so much that Darryl hardly r e _ _ _ _ i z e d her.

3. The _ _ _ u s c r i p t for the new book was more than one thousand pages.

4. Theresa gave her guests a very _ _ _ _ i a l welcome.

5. Bob likes to relax in his red r e _ _ _ _ _ _ r when he gets home from work.

6. The crosswalk was designed for the safety of _ _ _ e s t r i a n s.

7. The young couple _ _ _ a t e d a bag of clothing to the charity.

8. The doctor told Thomas that his disease was easily _ _ _ a b l e.

9. When Paul graduates from high school, he wants to join the _ _ _ i n e s.

10. Shannon's grandfather owned a large _ _ _ u f a c t u r i n g plant.

11. Unlike whales, most mammals are q u a d r u _ _ _ s.

44 CCSS: L.7.2b, L.7.4, L.7.4a, L.7.4b, L.7.6

© Saddleback Educational Publishing • www.sdlback.com
Common Core Skills & Strategies for Vocabulary: Level 7

NAME _____ DATE _____

LATIN ROOTS 2

Think about the words in which a root appears. Examples: luminous, illuminate, luminescent. The root lum must mean "light."

A. Directions: Circle the word that makes sense in each sentence.

1. *automobile, mobile, mobility*
   The root *mob* must mean (self / move / money).

2. *spectacle, spectator, inspect*
   The root *spec* must mean (see / glasses / sport).

3. *migrate, immigration, migratory*
   The root *migr* must mean (birds / people / move).

4. *fidelity, confidence, infidel*
   The root *fid* must mean (faith / sound / warrior).

5. *bellicose, belligerent, rebellion*
   The root *belli* must mean (calm / war / justice).

6. *community, communal, communism*
   The root *commun* must mean (political / inexpensive / common).

B. Directions: Read the meaning of the root and the example words. Then add one more word that contains this root.

ROOT	MEANING	EXAMPLES		
1. alt	high	*altitude*	*alto*	_____
2. grat	pleasing	*gratify*	*congratulate*	_____
3. doc	teach	*doctrine*	*doctor*	_____
4. pater	father	*paternal*	*patriarch*	_____

NAME _____ DATE _____

PREFIXES 1

A prefix *is a group of letters added to the beginning of a word to change its meaning.*

PREFIX	MEANING	EXAMPLE	PREFIX	MEANING	EXAMPLE
prot	first	protagonist	poly	many	polysyllabic
quint	five	quintet	bene	good	benefit
oct	eight	octagon	com	with	combine
extra	beyond	extracurricular	contra	against	contradict

Directions: Review the material in the chart above. Then use the prefixes to complete the words in the sentences. Use context clues for help.

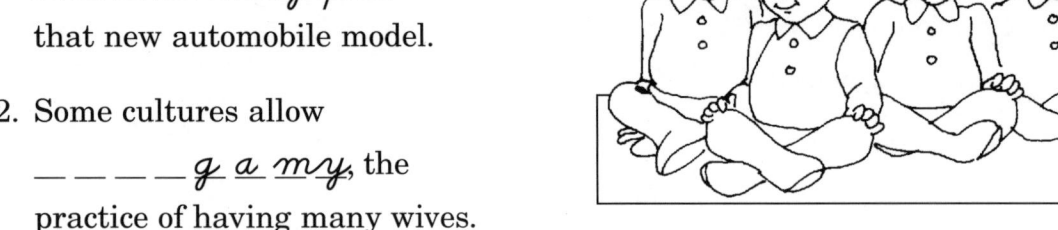

1. Chris designed the _ _ _ _ _ *otype* for that new automobile model.

2. Some cultures allow _ _ _ _ _ *gamy*, the practice of having many wives.

3. Diane is one of the famous _ _ _ _ _ *uplets* born in our city 15 years ago.

4. This particular medicine is _ _ _ _ _ _ _ *indicated* for your condition.

5. Our very generous _ _ _ _ _ *factor* prefers to remain anonymous.

6. Your friendship is a great joy and _ _ _ *fort* to me.

7. That talented girl has an _ _ _ _ _ _ *ordinary* singing voice.

8. Over the years, our jazz band has grown from a trio to an _ _ _ *et*.

9. A _ _ _ _ *nomial* is a math expression consisting of more than two terms.

10. The last church service of the day was a beautiful _ _ _ _ *diction*.

46 CCSS: L.7.2b, L.7.4, L.7.4a, L.7.4b, L.7.6

NAME _____   DATE _____

PREFIXES 2

How can you guess the meaning of a prefix? Think about the words in which it appears. Example: **midsummer, midway, midyear.** *The prefix* mid *must mean "middle."*

A. Directions: Circle the word that correctly completes each sentence.

1. *auto*matic, *auto*biography

    The prefix *auto* must mean
    (other / quick / **self**).

2. *im*balance, *im*mature

    The prefix *im* must mean
    (young / **not** / steady).

3. *pseudo*nym, *pseudo*classic

    The prefix *pseudo* must mean
    (**false** / true / old).

4. *mega*byte, *mega*ton

    The prefix *mega* must mean
    (small / **million** / loud).

5. *circu*mference, *circu*late

    The prefix *circu* must mean
    (area / air / **around**).

6. *micro*film, *micro*scope

    The prefix *micro* must mean
    (**small** / large / see).

B. Directions: The prefixes *en-* and *em-* both mean "in." Complete each word below with the correct prefix.

1. The two sisters __em__braced when they met at the family reunion.

2. Inez will __en__close a self-addressed, stamped envelope with her request.

3. The desperate bookkeeper decided to __em__bezzle money from her employer.

4. Emma likes to __em__broider her initials on her clothing.

5. Stu was __en__chanted by the beauty of his grandmother's old-fashioned garden.

6. Parents need to __en__courage their children to do their best.

NAME _____ DATE _____

SUFFIXES 1

A suffix *is a group of letters added to the end of a word to change its meaning. The suffixes in the box below indicate the "state" or "quality" of something.*

SUFFIX	EXAMPLE	SUFFIX	EXAMPLE	SUFFIX	EXAMPLE	SUFFIX	EXAMPLE
ancy	vacancy	**hood**	falsehood	**ization**	civilization	**ty**	loyalty
ery, ry	imagery	**ism**	heroism	**ude**	gratitude	**or**	error

Directions: Use the suffixes to complete the words in the sentences.

1. Luckily, the apartment building had a two-bedroom v a c _ _ _ _ _.

2. Silas faced every misfortune in his life with f o r t i _ _ _ _.

3. Sara and Erin are enjoying a very happy c h i l d _ _ _ _.

4. Over the years, the United States has suffered greatly because of r a c _ _ _.

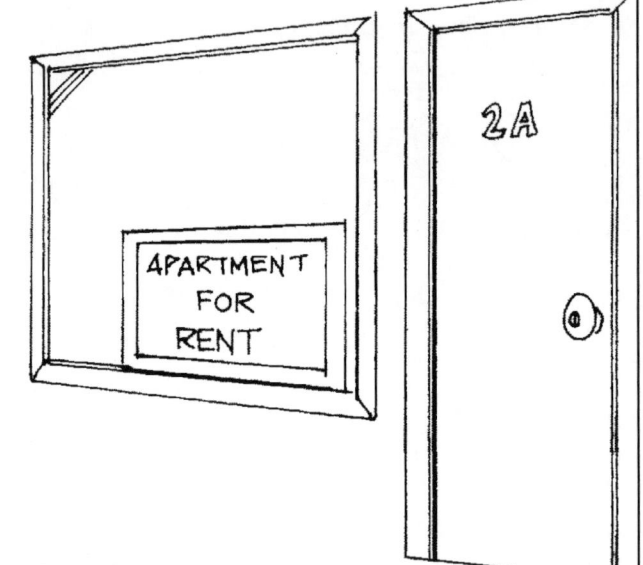

5. The poet e. e. cummings did not follow the rules of c a p i t a l _ _ _ _ _ _ _.

6. The reward for h o n e s _ _ is knowing that you did the right thing.

7. The p a l l _ _ in the sick child's face was quite alarming.

8. The soldier exhibited extreme b r a v e _ _ during the long battle.

9. The s t a n d a r d _ _ _ _ _ _ _ of shoe sizes makes it easy to buy footwear.

10. Heloise's belief in p a c i f _ _ _ prevents her from supporting any war.

11. The f e r v _ _ of his political ideas sets him apart from most people.

NAME _____ DATE _____

SUFFIXES 2

Many different suffixes have exactly the same meaning. This can be confusing, but give it your best try with the questions below.

A. Directions: Complete each word below with one of the **boldface** suffixes.

The *suffixes* **-al**, **-ary**, **-esque**, and **-ular** all mean "relating to."

1. her m a t e r n _ _ instincts
2. a tall and s t a t u _ _ _ _ _ model
3. a c i r c _ _ _ _ argument
4. full m i l i t _ _ _ honors
5. a p i c t u r _ _ _ _ _ scene
6. a p o p _ _ _ _ candidate
7. his n a t u r _ _ inclinations

B. Directions: Complete each word below with one of the **boldface** suffixes.

The *suffixes* **-ful**, **-ose**, **-ous**, and **-ulent** all mean "full of."

1. After watching the scary movie, the little boys were f e a r _ _ _ of the dark.
2. T u r b _ _ _ _ _ waves threatened to sink the small fishing boat.
3. Jeff was feeling n e r v _ _ _ before his job interview.
4. The accident victim was c o m a t _ _ _ for several days.
5. Rita is s u c c e s s _ _ _ at almost everything she tries.
6. The coronation of the young queen was truly g l o r i _ _ _.

NAME _____   DATE _____

NEAR MISSES 1

Some words can be confusing. They can look very much like a word that means something very different.

Directions: Circle the word that correctly completes each sentence. Use a dictionary for help, if necessary.

1. When moving cars have a (collision / collusion), both drivers and passengers can get hurt.

2. Over time, eating too much food will make your waistline (expend / expand).

3. After Myra lost so much weight, all her clothes were too (loose / lose).

4. The Martinez family told us they want to (adapt / adopt) a child.

5. After college, Beverly has decided to (pursue / peruse) a career in journalism.

6. Steven is in charge of the (personnel / personal) department in his company.

7. After running for three hours, Sylvia (finely / finally) crossed the finish line.

8. When it comes to books, Stanley has a (veracious / voracious) appetite.

9. Sue's many friends will continue to (perpetuate / perpetrate) her memory.

10. The lost hiker was hungry; he had been (depraved / deprived) of food for three days.

11. Caroline wrote information about her appointments on her (calendar / colander).

50 CCSS: L.7.3, L.7.4a

© Saddleback Educational Publishing • www.sdlback.com
Common Core Skills & Strategies for Vocabulary: Level 7

NAME _____ DATE _____

NEAR MISSES 2

A. Directions: Use eight of the *wrong* word choices in the previous exercise to complete the crossword puzzle.

ACROSS

3. fail to win

5. to commit (a crime)

7. to read or study

8. a secret agreement for a wrongful purpose

DOWN

1. a strainer

2. completely wicked

4. truthful

6. in an excellent manner

B. Directions: Write a letter to match each **boldface** "near miss" word with its meaning.

1. _____ **quite**   a. to look forward

2. _____ **quiet**   b. by means of

3. _____ **through**   c. relating to mankind

4. _____ **thorough**   d. very

5. _____ **expect**   e. kind

6. _____ **suspect**   f. to order

7. _____ **human**   g. not noisy

8. _____ **humane**   h. to praise

9. _____ **command**   i. complete

10. _____ **commend**   j. to mistrust

NAME _____   DATE _____

SYNONYMS: NOUNS 1

Synonyms *are words with the same or nearly the same meaning. The more synonyms you know, the richer your vocabulary will be.*

Directions: First write a letter to match each **boldface** noun with its synonym. Then find another synonym in the box for each pair of words. Write it on the line. Hint: You will not use all the words in the box. The first one has been done for you.

admission	cavity	exaggeration	haste
awning	comedy	flattery	hatred
ban	dwelling	glint	instructor

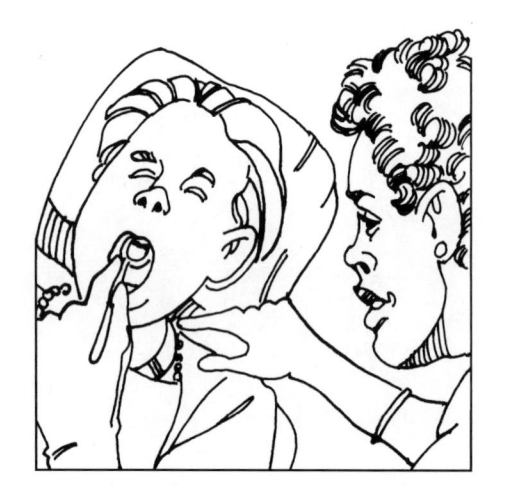

1. _b_ **affirmation**, _admission_   a. abode

2. ____ **pit**, _____   b. admittance

3. ____ **home**, _____   c. compliments

4. ____ **praise**, _____   d. elaboration

5. ____ **prohibition**, _____   e. hole

6. ____ **hyperbole**, _____   f. hurry

7. ____ **gleam**, _____   g. loathing

8. ____ **scramble**, _____   h. sparkle

9. ____ **abhorrence**, _____   i. taboo

10. ____ **professor**, _____   j. tutor

52   CCSS: L.7.1, L.7.2b, L.7.4a, L.7.4c, L.7.5b, L.7.5c, W.7.2d

NAME _____ DATE _____

SYNONYMS: NOUNS 2

Directions: Unscramble the *synonym* of the other **boldface** words in each sentence.

1. You carry a **(CACKURKS)** _____, or **knapsack**, the same way you carry a backpack.

2. If you want words meaning the same as **(GAMINICA)** _____, you could use **enchanter** or **necromancer**.

3. The team you're playing against could be called your **opponent**, **foe**, or **(MECIRTOPTO)** _____.

4. Victoria felt not only **excitement** and **emotion** for dancing—she had a real **(SONPIAS)** _____ for it.

5. When the **assault** began, those in the castle had no idea the **onslaught** would be even worse than the last **(GESIE)** _____.

6. The **(SRTOM)** _____ at sea began as a **squall** and quickly turned into a **tempest**.

7. We need a large **receptacle** for these flowers. Please get the blue **(ASEV)** _____ or the yellow **urn**.

8. The **lure** of the ocean was such an **attraction** for Sam that he gave in to the **(PITONETMAT)** _____ to buy a boat.

9. Before the trial, Myra gave a **statement**, or **declaration**. At the trial, she gave sworn **(SITOYMENT)** _____.

CCSS: L.7.1, L.7.2b, L.7.4a, L.7.4c, L.7.5b, L.7.5c, W.7.2d

NAME _____ DATE _____

SYNONYMS: VERBS 1

In a thesaurus, how many synonyms can find you for the word good?

A. Directions: Add an appropriate word from the box to each list of synonyms.
Hint: You will *not* use all the words in the box.

| admit | assure | catch | expel | induce | insult | invalidate | toss | uplift | waver |

1. _____
   taunt
   ridicule
   jeer

2. _____
   guarantee
   warrant
   pledge

3. _____
   initiate
   inaugurate
   introduce

4. _____
   falter
   fluctuate
   hesitate

5. _____
   cancel
   nullify
   repeal

6. _____
   acknowledge
   concede
   confess

7. _____
   grab
   snare
   capture

8. _____
   heave
   throw
   fling

9. _____
   banish
   exile
   deport

B. Directions: Now find two synonyms in the box for each **boldface** verb. Add the synonyms to each list. Hint: You will *not* use all the words.

appraise	burn	handy	deserve	harass	prefer	untwist
assess	char	curve	differ	justify	suitable	victimize
bend	choose	dawdle	digress	linger	untangle	

1. **merit**
   _____
   _____

2. **opt**
   _____
   _____

3. **persecute**
   _____
   _____

4. **unravel**
   _____
   _____

5. **scald**
   _____
   _____

6. **evaluate**
   _____
   _____

7. **convenient**
   _____
   _____

8. **vary**
   _____
   _____

9. **warp**
   _____
   _____

NAME _____ DATE _____

SYNONYMS: VERBS 2

A. Directions: First read each group of synonyms. Then unscramble the word that heads each list.

1. **EDAL** _____
   direct
   oversee
   supervise

2. **NAXIEME** _____
   observe
   scrutinize
   inspect

3. **VOREC** _____
   hide
   screen
   mask

4. **CHUNP** _____
   hit
   strike
   knock

5. **LOSI** _____
   stain
   dirt
   tarnish

6. **ROSUNURD** _____
   enclose
   encircle
   encompass

B. Directions: Write synonyms of your own for the following verbs.

1. sleep / _____
2. smudge / _____
3. reek / _____
4. lure / _____
5. influence / _____

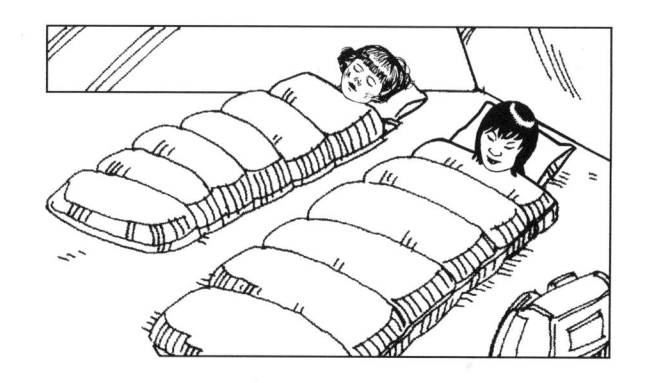

C. Directions: Now write original sentences using synonyms for these verbs: *cherish, cram, displease, intend, overcome, pose,* and *sulk.*

1. _____
2. _____
3. _____
4. _____
5. _____
6. _____
7. _____

NAME _____   DATE _____

SYNONYMS: ADJECTIVES 1

Here is some more synonym *practice. This time work with* adjectives *(describing words).*

Directions: First write a letter to match each **boldface** adjective with its synonym. Then find *another* synonym in the box for each pair of words. Write it on the line. Hint: You will *not* use all the words in the box. The first one has been done for you.

aged	ambitious	basic	miniature
changeable	received	flimsy	genuine
hardy	intellectual	irritated	irregular

1. _d_ **authenticated,** _genuine_   a. irked

2. ____ **elderly,** _____   b. cerebral

3. ____ **aspiring,** _____   c. accepted

4. ____ **bothered,** _____   d. validated

5. ____ **fragile,** _____   e. delicate

6. ____ **variable,** _____   f. diminutive

7. ____ **welcomed,** _____   g. old

8. ____ **tiny,** _____   h. strong

9. ____ **tough,** _____   i. hopeful

10. ____ **mental,** _____   j. differing

NAME _____ DATE _____

SYNONYMS: ADJECTIVES 2

A. Directions: Find two synonyms in the box for each **boldface** adjective. Write the synonyms on the lines. Hint: You will not use all the words in the box.

astute	dependable	dangerous	fancy	loyal	male
manly	pictorial	risky	scenic	sharp	showy
shriveled	triumphant	unique	unusual	uncontrollable	willful

1. **ornamental** shrubs
   _____
   _____

2. a **masculine** attitude
   _____
   _____

3. a **reliable** friend
   _____
   _____

4. a **treacherous** river
   _____
   _____

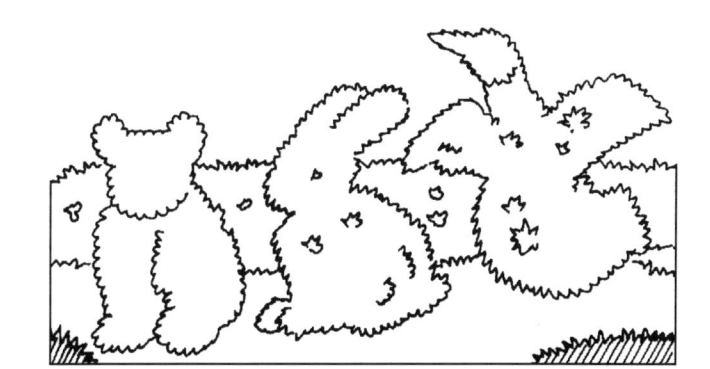

5. a **novel** approach
   _____
   _____

6. a **picturesque** location
   _____
   _____

B. Directions: Think of a synonym for each **boldface** adjective below. Write it on the line.

1. a **contagious** disease
   _____

2. a **feminine** trait
   _____

3. **delicious** foods
   _____

4. a **defiant** subject
   _____

5. an **exceptional** bargain
   _____

6. a **microscopic** speck
   _____

NAME _____ DATE _____

SYNONYMS: ADVERBS 1

Remember that an **adverb** *modifies or qualifies a verb, adjective, or another adverb. An adverb answers such questions as* **when? how? where? how often?** *and* **to what extent?**

A. Directions: Write a letter to match each **boldface** adverb with its synonym.

1. _____ **thankfully**   a. ably
2. _____ **accurately**   b. affectionately
3. _____ **quietly**   c. barely
4. _____ **lovingly**   d. correctly
5. _____ **skillfully**   e. craftily
6. _____ **slyly**   f. nearly
7. _____ **honestly**   g. silently
8. _____ **very**   h. gratefully
9. _____ **almost**   i. truthfully
10. _____ **hardly**   j. quite

B. Directions: Complete the crossword puzzle. Clues are synonyms of the answer words. Use the first letters as clues.

ACROSS

3. happily
6. definitely
8. entirely

DOWN

1. rarely
2. legibly
4. truly
5. forever
7. approximately

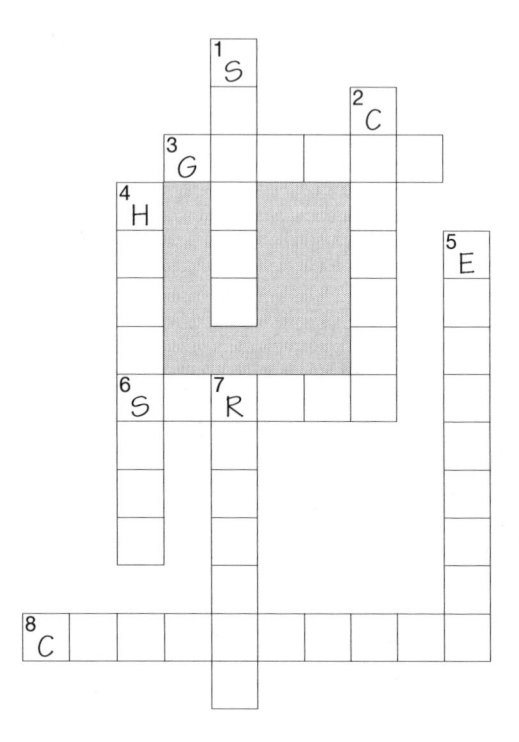

Crossword grid:
- 1 Down: S
- 2 Down: C
- 3 Across: G
- 4 Down: H
- 5 Down: E
- 6 Down: S
- 7 Down: R
- 8 Across: C

58   CCSS: L.7.1, L.7.2b, L.7.4a, L.7.4c, L.7.5b, L.7.5c, W.7.2d

© Saddleback Educational Publishing • www.sdlback.com
Common Core Skills & Strategies for Vocabulary: Level 7

NAME _____ DATE _____

SYNONYMS: ADVERBS 2

Directions: First unscramble the adverb in each sentence. Then circle its synonym.

1. Did you know that yo-yos were **(STRIF)** _____ used as weapons?

    never   originally

    often   seldom

2. That story you just told is **(TALTOLY)** _____ fantastic!

    entirely   partly

    almost   not

3. Gladys's clever new dance steps are **(MYSLIP)** _____ amazing!

    never   hardly   utterly   surprisingly

4. Justin **(NIBLDLY)** _____ joined in with whatever his friends were doing.

    happily   sadly   frequently   mindlessly

5. The careless electrician had made a **(YEVR)** _____ foolish error.

    quite   slightly   stupidly   almost

6. Almost **(LACITANCEDYL)** _____, the scientist made a great new discovery.

    overnight   immediately   wisely   mistakenly

7. The watermelon that won the contest was **(RETEXEMYL)** _____ large.

    greatly   slightly   moderately   almost

8. An **(SULALUNUY)** _____ fast car passed us on the freeway.

    barely   remarkably   hardly   dangerously

© Saddleback Educational Publishing • www.sdlback.com
Common Core Skills & Strategies for Vocabulary: Level 7
CCSS: L.7.1, L.7.2b, L.7.4a, L.7.4c, L.7.5b, L.7.5c, W.7.2d   59

NAME _____   DATE _____

ANTONYMS: NOUNS 1

The artful use of antonyms—words *with opposite meanings—can make your meanings crystal clear.*

A. Directions: Draw a line to match each **boldface** noun with its antonym.

1. **ally**   a. humility
2. **impatience**   b. calmness
3. **disturbance**   c. enemy
4. **pride**   d. success
5. **destruction**   e. creation
6. **disappointment**   f. patience

7. **endurance**   g. submission
8. **fad**   h. greeting
9. **struggle**   i. weakness
10. **farewell**   j. original
11. **imitation**   k. cruelty
12. **kindness**   l. convention

B. Directions: Use vowels *(a, e, i, o, u)* to complete the antonyms of the **boldface** nouns.

1. **laziness** / v _ g _ r
2. **leisure** / t _ _ l
3. **confusion** / c l _ r _ ty
4. **treason** / p _ t r _ _ t _ sm

5. **virtue** / _ v _ l
6. **youth** / m _ t _ r _ t y
7. **background** / f _ r _ g r _ _ n d
8. **seriousness** / j _ l l _ t y

C. Directions: Unscramble the antonyms. Then use each word in a sentence.

1. separation / **(TUINY)** _____ : _____

2. emotion / **(EONRAS)** _____ : _____

3. scoundrel / **(NAGLEMTEN)** _____ : _____

4. prudence / **(SHERSANS)** _____ : _____

NAME _____ DATE _____

ANTONYMS: NOUNS 2

A. Directions: Use the nouns in the box to make 14 pairs of antonyms.

B. Directions: Complete the crossword puzzle with antonyms of the clue words.

ACROSS
2. capture
5. loser
6. obscurity
7. attack

DOWN
1. smoothness
3. prosperity
4. ignorance

attic	courtesy	disrespect	heroism
cellar	dullness	hesitation	inclusion
brightness	hindrance	injustice	jobless
cowardice	elimination	flabbiness	importance
assistance	decision	employed	laughter
fairness	punishment	triviality	weeping
deflation	firmness	inflation	pardon

1. _____ / _____
2. _____ / _____
3. _____ / _____
4. _____ / _____
5. _____ / _____
6. _____ / _____
7. _____ / _____
8. _____ / _____
9. _____ / _____
10. _____ / _____
11. _____ / _____
12. _____ / _____
13. _____ / _____
14. _____ / _____

© Saddleback Educational Publishing • www.sdlback.com
Common Core Skills & Strategies for Vocabulary: Level 7
CCSS: L.7.1, L.7.2b, L.7.4a, L.7.5b   61

NAME _____   DATE _____

ANTONYMS: VERBS 1

Remember that **verbs** *are words that express an action, an occurrence, or a state of being.*

Directions: Circle the *antonym* of the **boldface** verb in each sentence.

1. Cynthia decided to **increase** the time she spends practicing ballet.

    enjoy   lengthen   justify   abbreviate

2. The counselor told the young campers to **join** hands.

    hold   wash   disconnect   massage

3. After a long, drawn-out trial, the prisoner was finally **exonerated**.

    convicted   shackled   questioned   honored

4. Stanley bravely tried to **banish** all frightening thoughts from his mind.

    hide   welcome   forget   remember

5. Some people believe that opposites **attract**.

    repel   connect   show off   communicate

6. The babysitter **entertained** the restless little boys for four hours.

    danced   pampered   ignored   watched

7. The rebel forces **imprisoned** their captive for five long months.

    tortured   questioned   nourished   released

8. The condition of the infected tooth gradually **worsened** over the weekend.

    improved   ached   diminished   deteriorated

9. After fitting the new pipe, the plumber **tightened** the bolts.

    sold   attached   loosened   checked

NAME _____ DATE _____

ANTONYMS: VERBS 2

A. Directions: Unscramble the word to complete each pair of *antonyms*.

1. depart / **(REAVRI)** _____

2. defrost **(EREFEZ)** _____

3. isolate **(NIDCULE)** _____

4. resist / **(BUSTIM)** _____

5. pity / **(NEVY)** _____

6. evade / **(CAPARPHO)** _____

7. purchase / **(LESL)** _____

8. allow / **(DIBROF)** _____

9. esteem / **(COMK)** _____

10. display / **(OCANCEL)** _____

B. Directions: Complete the crossword puzzle with antonyms of the clue words. Use the first letters as clues.

ACROSS
2. flatten
4. agree
7. begin
8. complicate

DOWN
1. soften
3. bore
5. cover
6. fire

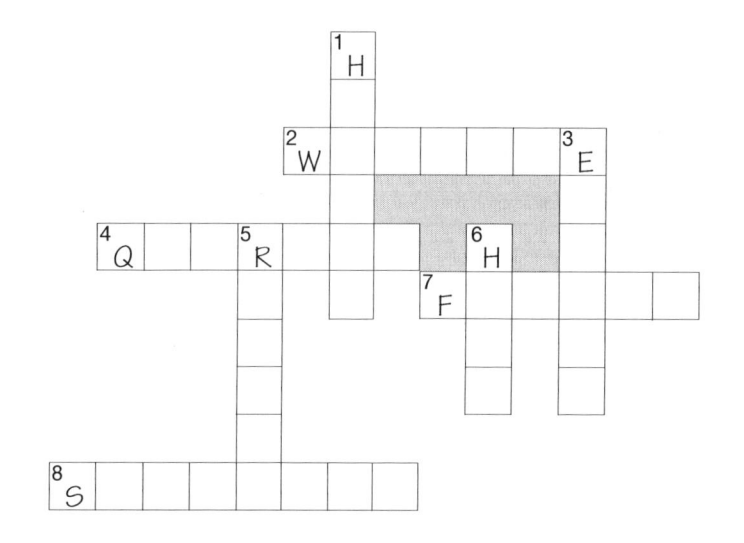

© Saddleback Educational Publishing • www.sdlback.com
Common Core Skills & Strategies for Vocabulary: Level 7
CCSS: L.7.1, L.7.2b, L.7.4a, L.7.5b   63

NAME _____ DATE _____

ANTONYMS: ADJECTIVES 1

You already know that adjectives *describe nouns and pronouns. But do you also know that adjectives often tell* how many *or* what kind?

A. Directions: Add vowels *(a, e, i, o, u)* to complete the antonyms of the **boldface** adjectives.

1. Casual clothes are all right for regular school dances, but the prom is a f _ rm _ l affair.

2. That puppy is very active, but this one seems very p _ ss _ v _.

3. We had to replace the warped board with a st r _ _ ght one.

4. This undervalued antique was once a little girl's ch _ r _ sh _ d doll.

5. Saul was embarrassed about his act at the talent show, but Roger was p r _ _ d of his.

6. Is Elizabeth's playmate an actual one or an _ m _ g _ n _ ry one?

7. We wanted a secluded campsite, but all we could find was a c r _ wd _ d area.

8. The native population resented the influx of the _ l _ _ n intruders.

B. Directions: Find an antonym in the box for each adjective below. Write it on the line.

| bound | comfortable | delicate | elongated | harmless | lowered | optimistic | resistant |

1. **yielding** / _____
2. **tough** / _____
3. **shortened** / _____
4. **elevated** / _____
5. **uneasy** / _____
6. **loose** / _____
7. **injurious** / _____
8. **pessimistic** / _____

NAME _____ DATE _____

ANTONYMS: ADJECTIVES 2

A. Directions: Unscramble the adjectives to complete each pair of *antonyms*.

1. cheerful / (**LOYGOM**) _____

2. internal / (**TENLERAX**) _____

3. rare / (**MOCNOM**) _____

4. original / (**PEDCIO**) _____

5. extended / (**EBIRF**) _____

6. logical / (**LARAINIROT**) _____

7. obedient / (**RULNUY**) _____

8. incompetent / (**LEAB**) _____

9. righteous / (**LETUHICAN**) _____

10. deficient / (**ETAQADUE**) _____

B. Directions: Complete the crossword puzzle with antonyms of the **boldface** clue words.

ACROSS

4. a **lively** participant

6. your **truthful** eyes

7. **dainty** material

DOWN

1. a **generous** fellow

2. the **hydrated** plant

3. **vulgar** manners

5. an **unscrupulous** decision

Crossword grid clues visible:
- 1: S
- 2: P
- 3: R
- 4: I
- 5: M
- 6: L
- 7: C

CCSS: L.7.1, L.7.2b, L.7.4a, L.7.5b

NAME _____   DATE _____

ANTONYMS: ADVERBS 1

Remember that adverbs *modify verbs, adjectives, or other adverbs.*

A. Directions: Find an *antonym* (word that means the opposite) in the box for each **boldface** adverb. Write it on the line. Hint: You will *not* use all the words.

| abruptly | angrily | briskly | unhappily | foolishly |
| accidentally | brightly | certainly | often | thoughtfully |

1. Jeremy said goodbye to Alexis very **slowly** (_____).
2. Janice very **wisely** (_____) refrained from overeating.
3. Emma **seldom** (_____) goes to the movies.
4. Homer looked up **dully** (_____) and said, "Huh?"
5. On hot days, Monica moves very **sluggishly** (_____).
6. When asked if he would get an A on the test, Al said, "**Doubtfully**." (_____).
7. After her long vacation, Amanda **joyfully** (_____) returned home.
8. Dustin **purposely** (_____) turned off the computer.
9. Dana **selfishly** (_____) kept all the good peaches for himself.

B. Directions: Complete the puzzle with antonyms of the **boldface** adverbs.

ACROSS

3. behaves **indifferently**
5. **partly** responsible
6. treated **roughly**
7. acted **sanely**

DOWN

1. **indistinctly** visible
2. **busily** at work
4. greeted **courteously**
5. **unjustly** angry

66 CCSS: L.7.1, L.7.2b, L.7.4a, L.7.5b

NAME _____ DATE _____

ANTONYMS: ADVERBS 2

A. Directions: Sort the adverbs in the box to make six pairs of *antonyms* (words with opposite meanings). Write them on the lines. See the example.

angrily	awkwardly	definitely
sometimes	famously	gracefully
commonly	invariably	patiently
obscurely	unusually	questionably

1. *angrily*
   patiently
2. _____
3. _____
4. _____
5. _____
6. _____

B. Directions: Complete the crossword puzzle with antonyms of the **boldface** adverbs. Use the first letters as clues.

ACROSS

1. **Fortunately**, he won.
6. She spoke **sweetly**.
7. He landed the plane **dangerously**.
8. **Sometimes** she danced.
9. They moved **quickly**.

DOWN

2. I treated him **kindly**.
3. Hank spoke **distinctly**.
4. She's **rarely** in a good mood.
5. Sue played **energetically**.

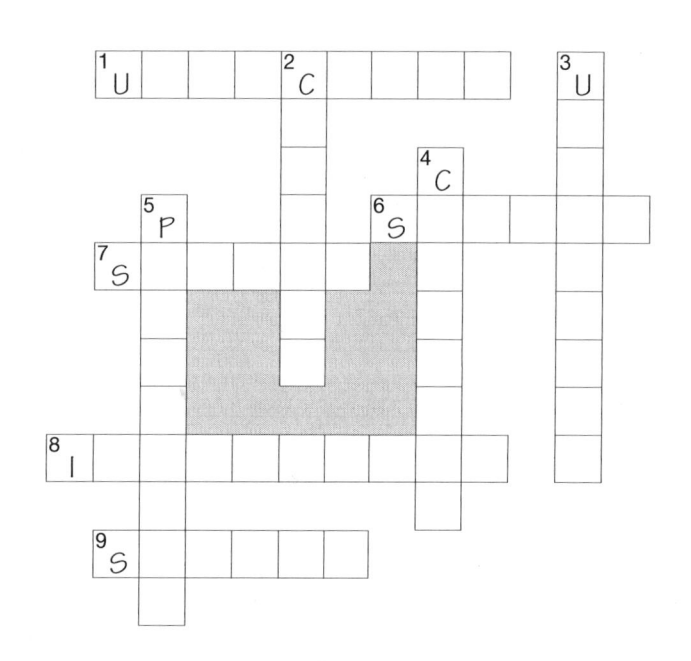

Crossword clues: 1-U, 2-C, 3-U, 4-C, 5-P, 6-S, 7-S, 8-I, 9-S

© Saddleback Educational Publishing • www.sdlback.com
Common Core Skills & Strategies for Vocabulary: Level 7   CCSS: L.7.1, L.7.2b, L.7.4a, L.7.5b   67

NAME _____   DATE _____

HOMOPHONES

Homophones *are words that sound alike but are spelled differently and have different meanings. Some examples of homophones are* **be/bee** *and* **flour/flower.**

A. Directions: Say the words aloud. Then write a homophone next to each word.

1. allowed / _____   4. ball / _____   7. sent / _____
2. crews / _____   5. find / _____   8. main / _____
3. lie / _____   6. meet / _____   9. one / _____

B. Directions: Complete the crossword puzzle with homophones for the **boldface** words.

ACROSS

2. a sincere **compliment**
4. belongs to **him**
5. everyone **who's** here
7. a freshly **mown** lawn
8. **pour** the milk
9. **shoot** the breeze
10. going **away**

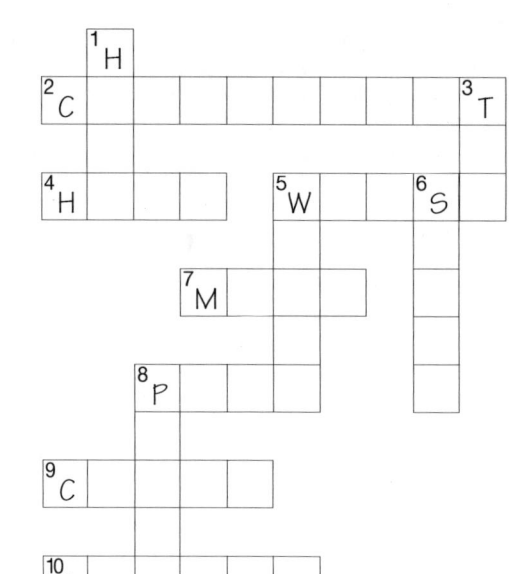

DOWN

1. a **holey** shirt
3. a cup of **tea**
5. all **we've** been doing
6. the lights **shone** brightly
8. a cat's **paws**

C. Directions: Circle three homophone errors in each sentence. Then rewrite the sentences correctly on the lines.

1. The buoy climbed up the fur tree and the beach tree.

   _____

2. After the accident, wee set off fore flairs to get attention.

   _____

68   CCSS: L.7.3, L.7.4a, L.7.6

NAME _____ DATE _____

HOMOPHONE RIDDLES

Figure out these riddles by using your imagination and your sense of humor.

EXAMPLE: What would you call a music group that is no longer allowed to play music? a <u>banned band</u>

A. Directions: Use vowels *(a, e, i, o, u)* to fill in the blanks.

What would you call . . .

1. a poet in jail? b_rr_d b_rd

2. a dog's sound on a boat? b_rq__ b_rk

3. a container for cotton pods? b_ll b_wl

4. a variety of breakfast food day after day? s_r__l c_r__l

5. corn for military higher-ups? k_rn_ls for c_l_n_ls

6. a medieval jouster who doesn't like the daytime? n_ght kn_ght

7. a greeting from someone in a hot-air balloon? a h_gh h_

B. Directions: Now solve the riddles by using only the first letters as clues.

What would you call . . .

1. a monk who cooks chicken? f_____ f_____
2. an unfriendly, cheap youth hotel? h_____ h_____
3. a dish full of supplies for making braids? p_____ p_____
4. a seer who tells the future for money? p_____ for p_____
5. a colorless bucket? p_____ p_____
6. a picturesque view that was observed? s_____ s_____

NAME _____   DATE _____

HOMOGRAPHS

Words that are spelled alike but have different meanings are called **homographs.**

EXAMPLE: *baste* 1. to pour liquid on while roasting; 2. to sew with long stitches

A. Directions: Unscramble the homographs that match each definition below. The first one has been done for you.

1. **(TUCERON)** _counter_ :
   a. one who counts
   b. long table in a store or restaurant

2. **(INEP)** _____ :
   a. to yearn or long for
   b. a type of evergreen

3. **(MODCUNOP)** _____ :
   a. having more than one part
   b. an enclosed yard

4. **(WOBL)** _____ :
   a. a hard hit
   b. send forth a stream of air

5. **(ENFI)** _____ :
   a. high quality
   b. money paid as punishment

6. **(DEHI)** _____ :
   a. to conceal; keep out of sight
   b. animal skin

B. Directions: Write homographs to find the answer to the riddle (reads top to bottom). Use the definitions as clues. The first one has been done for you.

RIDDLE: *Homographs have the same spelling but different meanings and* _____ .

1. bubbling of hot liquid; red swelling on the skin
2. container made of glass; to rattle or vibrate
3. container for pouring liquid; baseball player
4. one side of a sheet of paper; youth who runs errands
5. friendly and helpful; same type or class
6. opposite of *up*; soft feathers
7. newly made, not stale; impudent, bold

1. _b_ _o_ _i_ _l_
2. _ _ _ _
3. _ _ _ _ _ _
4. _ _ _ _
5. _ _ _ _
6. _ _ _ _
7. _ _ _ _ _

NAME _____ DATE _____

HOMOPHONES AND HOMOGRAPHS: DICTIONARY PRACTICE

Remember these definitions:
- **Homophones** *are words that* sound *exactly alike but have different spellings and meanings.*
- **Homographs** *are words that* look *exactly alike but have different* meanings.

A. Directions: First write the *homophone* for each **boldface** word. Then write a brief definition of the homophone you added. Check a dictionary if you need help.

1. Sheila has a new **beau**. _____ : _____

2. The ref **blew** the whistle. _____ : _____

3. Hal removed the apple **core**. _____ : _____

4. The horses ate **hay**. _____ : _____

5. The **lesson** took 50 minutes. _____ : _____

B. Directions: Write two sentences showing each meaning of the **boldface** *homographs.* The first one has been done for you. Check a dictionary if you need help.

1. **carp** (verb) *If you carp about something, you complain about it.*
   carp (noun) *A carp is an edible fish found in fresh water.*

2. **chuck** (noun) _____
   chuck (verb) _____

3. **hatch** (noun) _____
   hatch (verb) _____

NAME _____ DATE _____

CLIPPED WORDS 1

A clipped *word is one that has been shortened by common use, such as "trike" instead of "tricycle."*

A. Directions: Write out the complete form of the clipped words shown in **boldface**. Check a dictionary if you're not sure.

1. buy a new **auto**
   _____

2. a young **coed**
   _____

3. the study of **trig**
   _____

4. a **deli** sandwich
   _____

5. one **cent** in change
   _____

6. a **cuke** for your salad
   _____

7. go underwater in a **sub**
   _____

8. wear a **wig**
   _____

B. Directions: Now write the clipped form of each **boldface** word or words.

1. a talented **veterinarian** _____

2. a **typographical** error _____

3. go out to **luncheon** _____

4. an attractive **debutante** _____

5. see the **doctor** _____

6. a **modern** hair style _____

7. wearing tailored **pantaloons** _____

8. an arrangement of **chrysanthemums** _____

NAME _____ DATE _____

CLIPPED WORDS 2

A. Directions: Solve the crossword puzzle. Answers are the complete forms of the **boldface** clipped words.

ACROSS

3. wore a tie and **tails**
4. told the pest to **scram**
5. brewed in a **still**
6. wore thick **specs**
7. coffee began to **perk**

DOWN

1. **lube** the engine
2. sit around and **gab**

B. Directions: Use vowels *(a, e, i, o, u)* to complete the longer form of each **boldface** clipped word.

1. The only job Jacob could get was as a taxicab **hack**. h _ c k n _ y

2. Barbara bought a new **curio** cabinet. c _ r _ _ s _ t y

3. Larry went to see a **movie**. m _ v _ n g p _ c t _ r _

4. The criminal had spent many years in the **pen**.

   p _ n _ t _ n t _ _ r y

5. Theresa drove 40 miles on the **pike**. t _ r n p _ k _

6. Donald is on the **varsity** football team. _ n _ v _ r s _ t y

7. Caroline and Richard went to the **prom** together. p r _ m _ n _ d _

NAME _____   DATE _____

WORDS BORROWED FROM NAMES 1

Many English words had their origins in the names of people and places. For example, cashmere, a fine wool fabric, is named for the goats of Kashmir, India, whose downy wool is used in the manufacture of this product.

A. Directions: Write a letter to match each **boldface** word with its origin.

1. _____ **argyle**
2. _____ **cologne**
3. _____ **doily**
4. _____ **frankfurter**
5. _____ **manila paper**
6. _____ **quisling**
7. _____ **sandwich**
8. _____ **suede**

a. named after the Scottish clan Campbell of Argyll, Scotland

b. named by the French after the Swedish inventor of this type of leather

c. named for the German city of Cologne, which in turn was named after Colonia Agrippina, the Roman empress who was born there

d. named after the hemp made in Manila, the Philippines, from which it was originally made

e. named after Vidkun Quisling, a Norwegian who was shot for treason after World War II

f. named after the city of Frankfurt, Germany

g. named after John Montagu, fourth Earl of Sandwich, who invented it so he could continue gambling without stopping for a normal meal

h. named for a person named Doily or Doyley, who kept a shop in London in the late 17th century

B. Directions: Look up the origins of these words and write them on the lines.

1. **tabby** _____
2. **martinet** _____
3. **diesel** _____
4. **dunce** _____
5. **guillotine** _____

WORDS BORROWED FROM NAMES 2

The names of places, people, and even gods form the basis of many English words.

Directions: Use the clues to complete the crossword puzzle.

ACROSS

3. Amelia Bloomer, a pioneer feminist, made this garment popular.
5. Atlas was a Titan in Greek myth. In the front of books of maps, he was often pictured holding up the earth.
6. A man named Beaulieu, a famous hatter of the mid-19th century, designed this hat that has a low crown.
11. Louis Pasteur invented the process by which we do this to our milk to kill bacteria.
12. This day of the week is named after Fria, the Norse goddess of love and beauty.

7. Teddy Roosevelt was the U.S. president who spared the life of a bear cub on a hunting trip in Mississippi. (2 words)
8. The Italian physicist Alessandro Volta named this unit for measuring the force of an electrical current.
9. This soft knitted cloth was originally made in Jersey, a British island in the English Channel.
10. This month was named for the Roman goddess Maia.

DOWN

1. This month is named after Julius Caesar.
2. These crackers are named after their inventor, Sylvester Graham. (2 words)
4. Samuel Maverick, a Texan who didn't brand his cattle, gives us this word for someone who doesn't follow the crowd.

NAME _____ DATE _____

FOREIGN WORDS AND PHRASES 1

Many words and phrases from other languages have found their way into the English language.

Directions: Use context clues to help you figure out the meaning of the **boldface** words and phrases. Check a dictionary if you need help. Circle a letter to show your answer.

1. "**Entre nous**," said Yvonne as a warning to Emma to keep the information secret.
   a. or else
   b. now or never
   c. between ourselves

2. When Allison saw the **trompe-l'oeil** design on the wall, she thought she was looking down a long hallway.
   a. optical illusion
   b. checkerboard
   c. oil paint

3. Ross purchased a **pied-à-terre** so he wouldn't have to pay hotel bills when he visited the city.
   a. minivan with television monitors
   b. apartment maintained for convenience
   c. hotel pass good for a year

4. Andy had a moment of **déjà vu**. "I know we've met before," he said.
   a. a feeling that something strange is about to happen
   b. the illusion of having experienced something previously
   c. the wish to impress strangers

5. The **crudités** served at the party were healthful in themselves, but the dips were full of fat.
   a. raw vegetables
   b. chips
   c. drinks

6. Sammy was proud to see his name included in the **dramatis personae** of the play.
   a. advertisers
   b. cast of characters
   c. stagehands and assistants

7. This wonderful weather seems to invite us to dine **al fresco**.
   a. on light food
   b. in a leisurely manner
   c. outdoors

76   CCSS: L.7.4, L.7.4a

© Saddleback Educational Publishing • www.sdlback.com
Common Core Skills & Strategies for Vocabulary: Level 7

FOREIGN WORDS AND PHRASES 2

Do you want to be a rara avis? One way to do it is to learn and use these foreign expressions.

Directions: Write a letter to match each **boldface** word or phrase with its meaning. Check a dictionary if you're not sure.

1. _____ As Shirley served the magnificent meal, she said, "**Bon appétit!**" to her guests.

2. _____ Believing that art should imitate life, Brian prefers **cinéma vérité** to fantasy.

3. _____ If you are asked to respond to an invitation, it is **de rigueur** that you do so.

4. _____ Maureen graduated **summa cum laude** from the university.

5. _____ Theodore, wanting to squeeze the most out of life, lives by the motto "**Carpe diem!**"

6. _____ Edith is a **rara avis** who is comfortable among all sorts of people.

7. _____ Brad told us about his vacation in all its boring details, **ad nauseum**.

8. _____ Carol acted **in loco parentis** for her foster child.

9. _____ Despite their difficulties, Karl and Linda smiled and said "**Omnia vincit amor!**"

10. _____ Asked if she wanted to shop, Laurie said, "**Au contraire.** I have decided to save my money!"

11. _____ Jacob repeated his conversation with Antoine **verbatim**.

a. Eat well!

b. in the place of a parent

c. Love conquers all!

d. on and on; to the point of disgust

e. on the contrary

f. rare bird; unusual person

g. realistic films

h. required by the rules of etiquette

i. Seize the day!

j. with highest honors

k. word for word

NAME _____   DATE _____

SIMPLE IDIOMS 1

All languages have idioms—expressions that have special meanings. The words in idioms are not meant to be taken literally. For example, to "spill the beans" means to tell a secret to someone who is not supposed to know about it.

A. Directions: Circle a letter to show the meaning of the **boldface** idiom.

1. Call if you need me, because I can come **at the drop of a hat**.
   a. immediately
   b. in about an hour
   c. after I get dressed

2. At her new job, Stella was **at sea** for the first few weeks.
   a. on a business trip
   b. on vacation
   c. confused

3. To **break the ice**, Minerva suggested a game of charades.
   a. go ice-skating
   b. get the party started
   c. chop a block of ice

4. That bully keeps all the younger children **under his thumb**.
   a. controlled by him
   b. protected by him
   c. helped by him

B. Directions: Write a letter to match each **boldface** idiom on the left with its meaning on the right.

1. _____ to **branch out**
2. _____ to **break one's heart**
3. _____ to **fly off the handle**
4. _____ to **make up one's mind**
5. _____ to **do the honors**
6. _____ to **get through to**
7. _____ to **keep one's chin up**
8. _____ to **nip in the bud**

a. to act as host or hostess
b. to add new interests or activities
c. to be understood
d. to become very angry
e. to block in the beginning
f. to choose what to do
g. to make very sad
h. to face trouble with courage

78 CCSS: L.7.4, L.7.4a, L.7.5, L.7.5a, L.7.6

© Saddleback Educational Publishing • www.sdlback.com
Common Core Skills & Strategies for Vocabulary: Level 7

NAME _____ DATE _____

SIMPLE IDIOMS 2

Directions: Circle the idiom that correctly completes each sentence.

1. Diane (carried on / carried off) with her career in ballet.

2. When asked what the capital of Afghanistan was, Sam (drew a conclusion / drew a blank).

3. On "casual Fridays," people in our office are allowed to (dress down / dress up).

4. Stella is a good example to her younger sister, who has always (looked down on / looked up to) her.

5. The banker (lost heart / lost face) with his clients when they found out he had a gambling problem.

6. Because of rising costs in other areas, the state had to (cut back / cut in) on health coverage.

7. Although they usually agreed, Lulu and Frank did not (see the light / see eye to eye) on this one thing.

8. Aunt Marie decided to (take on / take out) the job of caring for her nephew.

9. A good education is the first step if you want to (get ahead / get around).

10. Dolores (kept down / kept at) her project until she finished it.

NAME _____ DATE _____

INTERPRETING IDIOMS 1

Remember that idioms are not meant to be taken literally.

Directions: Circle a letter to show the meaning of each **boldface** idiom.

1. Melinda likes to **catch some rays** at the beach on Sundays.
   a. look for manta rays in the water
   b. get tanned while sunbathing
   c. play a game of catch

2. Everyone knows that grouchy woman's **bark is worse than her bite**.
   a. sound is more frightening than actions
   b. has a loud dog
   c. bad temper doesn't last long

3. Business has improved since the restaurant **changed hands**.
   a. hired new servers
   b. got new equipment
   c. transferred ownership

4. When Mark tried to take over Steve's job, he found himself **in deep water**.
   a. in serious difficulty
   b. working as a lifeguard
   c. in a good position

5. I never tell Lisa any secrets because she likes to **dish the dirt**.
   a. work in the garden
   b. clean house
   c. gossip

6. Twyla is **down to the wire** on her term paper.
   a. running out of time
   b. proud of
   c. not happy with

7. That money will be **down the drain** if you lend it to Chuck.
   a. in the sink
   b. lost
   c. wisely invested

8. Tommy Wilson is a **dyed-in-the-wool** Democrat.
   a. being pressured
   b. threatening others
   c. committed

80 CCSS: L.7.4, L.7.4a, L.7.5, L.7.5a, L.7.6

NAME _____   DATE _____

INTERPRETING IDIOMS 2

Directions: Circle a letter to show the meaning of each **boldface** idiom.

1. By saying she felt **fit as a fiddle**, Maria meant that

    a. she wanted to play some music.

    b. she was overweight.

    c. she was in very good health.

2. If you use **elbow grease** to get a room clean, you use

    a. physical labor and effort.

    b. soap and water.

    c. special equipment.

3. The comedian knew that his joke **fell flat** when

    a. everyone laughed.

    b. no one laughed.

    c. the microphone stopped working.

4. When Tyrone said he'd go out with Alice, **Dutch treat**, he meant that

    a. he would treat her.

    b. he'd pay his own way, and Alice would pay hers.

    c. they would have to walk to the restaurant.

5. When Manny ran **full tilt** into the door and broke his nose, he was running

    a. at high speed.

    b. slowly.

    c. without looking where he was going.

6. Some girls wanted to fight Sandra, but she **gave them the slip** when she

    a. beat them up first.

    b. passed them a note.

    c. escaped from them.

7. When Amanda told John to **go jump in the lake**, she meant that he should

    a. go away and stop being a bother.

    b. go take a good swim.

    c. take some time to go fishing.

8. When Louisa **let her hair down** at the party, she

    a. undid her braids.

    b. relaxed and had some fun.

    c. got a haircut.

NAME _____   DATE _____

EXPLAINING IDIOMS 1

Idioms are the hardest part of a language to learn. Why? Because the words don't mean what they normally do. But idioms can add a great deal of color to what you say.

Directions: Circle a letter to correctly answer each question.

What actually happened if...

1. You had a **bee in your bonnet**?
    a. You got stung by a bee.
    b. You had a fixed idea that seemed odd.
    c. You bought some honey.

2. You **bad mouthed** someone?
    a. You hit him or her.
    b. You gave him or her some spoiled food.
    c. You spoke badly of him or her.

3. You were **at loggerheads** with your neighbors?
    a. You had a quarrel.
    b. You mended a fence.
    c. You stacked firewood.

4. You were **called on the carpet**?
    a. You got scolded or reprimanded.
    b. You bought a new rug.
    c. You slept on the floor.

5. You **called the tune**?
    a. You sang a song.
    b. You acted as a disc jockey at a party.
    c. You gave orders or directions.

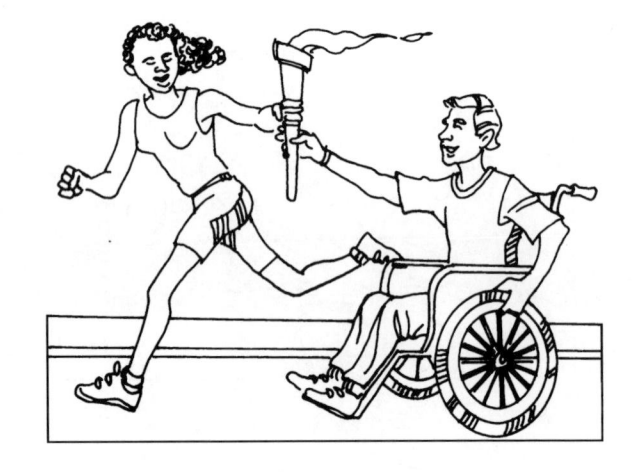

6. You **carried a torch** for someone?
    a. You lit candles.
    b. You fell in love.
    c. You held a flashlight.

7. You **kept your nose clean**?
    a. You stayed out of trouble.
    b. You took frequent baths.
    c. You avoided getting colds.

8. You **painted yourself into a corner**?
    a. You painted a floor from the outside in.
    b. You got into a difficult situation.
    c. You got out of a difficult situation.

82   CCSS: L.7.4, L.7.4a, L.7.5, L.7.5a, L.7.6

© Saddleback Educational Publishing • www.sdlback.com
Common Core Skills & Strategies for Vocabulary: Level 7

NAME _____ DATE _____

EXPLAINING IDIOMS 2

A. Directions: Write the word that correctly completes each **boldface** idiom.

1. When Zach told Celeste about the insurance settlement, she warned him not to count his _____ **before they hatch**.

    money   robins   chickens   birds

2. The children **dragged their** _____ when their mother sent them to bed.

    teddy bears   feet   books   pajamas

3. Scarlett was **head over** _____ in love with Rhett.

    heart   feet   shoulders   heels

4. To get this job, you will have to **jump through many** _____.

    hoops   windows   doors   puddles

5. "I'd like to **pick your** _____ about computers," said Frankie.

    pocket   brain   time   attitude

B. Directions: Draw a line to connect each idiom with its meaning.

A person who is . . .

1. **blowing the whistle** is   a. having a conversation.

2. **shooting the breeze** is   b. informing against a law-breaker.

3. **quitting cold turkey** is   c. past his or her prime.

4. **going overboard** is   d. suddenly stopping a bad habit.

5. **over the hill** is   e. wildly enthusiastic.

NAME _____ DATE _____

USING IDIOMS IN CONTEXT 1

You can often figure out the meaning of common idioms by using context clues.

Directions: Circle a letter to complete each sentence with the correct idiom.

1. Ernest knew he had done wrong, so he decided to _____ and take his punishment.
   a. face down
   b. face the music
   c. fall flat

2. Because Jim wanted the car so badly, he was willing to
   a. hit pay dirt.
   b. pass the buck.
   c. pay through the nose.

3. To describe the members of a close family, you might say they are
   a. close to home.
   b. close-knit.
   c. a closed book.

4. Allison didn't like Janet's company, so she gave her
   a. the cold shoulder.
   b. a cold fish.
   c. cold feet.

5. Because Jake doesn't get nervous in difficult situations, he can be described as
   a. hot under the collar.
   b. over the top.
   c. cool as a cucumber.

6. A small payment on a large bill might be called
   a. a drop in the bucket.
   b. duck soup.
   c. easy money.

7. A person who is inexperienced or innocent in worldly things is called a
   a. babe in the woods.
   b. fair-haired boy.
   c. big daddy.

8. Sara and Erin are so similar that people say they are like
   a. water off a duck's back.
   b. two peas in a pod.
   c. little frogs in big ponds.

84 CCSS: L.7.4, L.7.4a, L.7.5, L.7.5a, L.7.6

© Saddleback Educational Publishing • www.sdlback.com
Common Core Skills & Strategies for Vocabulary: Level 7

NAME _____ DATE _____

USING IDIOMS IN CONTEXT 2

Directions: Select two appropriate idioms from the box to complete each sentence. Write the idioms on the lines.

turned a deaf ear to	make ends meet	come clean
lay down the law	hit the nail on the head	make up for
fall short	hold a candle to	playing second fiddle
get away with	pull strings	take it easy
have it both ways	eating them out of house and home	

1. Because June couldn't _____ Margaret, she was used to _____ when she was with her.

2. Their grown son was _____, so they had to _____ and order him to get a job.

3. It's impossible for Charlie to _____ on the weekends because he can't really _____ unless he works two jobs.

4. After their quarrel, Inez tried to _____ and apologize, but Cynthia _____ her.

5. To _____ all the times he'd let Fernando down, Eddie decided to _____ to help him get a good job.

6. You have unfortunately _____ by saying that we will _____ of this week's goals.

7. You cannot _____; it's impossible to _____ _____ your deceptions any longer.

NAME _____   DATE _____

A-B WORDS IN CONTEXT 1

Words that begin with A and B can add attitude and boldness to your vocabulary.

Directions: Complete the sentences with words from the box. Hint: You will *not* use all the words. Check a dictionary if you need help.

ability
abrasive
absorb
accelerate
accessory
adhere
aerobics
agenda
barge
barnacles
belated
brocade
bronchitis
buoyant

1. Anna very much enjoys her _____ classes at the gym.

2. Aunt Elaine forgot Jerry's birthday, so she sent him a _____ birthday card.

3. Carl wants to be a ship's captain some day, but for now he loads freight on a river _____.

4. If the bottom of the ship isn't cleaned often, _____ will attach themselves to it.

5. Sylvia's shawl is made of a fine _____ woven with gold and silver threads.

6. A chameleon has the _____ to change its color to match the environment.

7. This car does not _____ fast enough to enter the freeway safely.

8. This paper towel can _____ much more water than that one.

9. Your new silver belt is the perfect _____ for that outfit.

10. You need special glue to make the pieces _____ to plywood.

11. If a soap is _____ it is much easier to find it in the bathtub.

12. "What's on our _____ for today?" Phil asked his partner.

NAME _____ DATE _____

A-B WORDS IN CONTEXT 2

Directions: Read the definitions of the A-B words. Then use each word in an original sentence.

accuracy freedom from all errors or mistakes
acknowledge to recognize the authority or claims of
adjourn to stop a meeting, etc. with the intention of beginning again later
affinity a natural attraction or liking
banish to force to leave a country, as by political decree
blackmail to get money or a service from, by threatening to tell something damaging
boundary something, as a line or mark, that forms an outer limit, edge, or extent
bureaucracy government with many departments made up of appointed officials, who follow set rules and regulations
buttress a structure built against a wall to strengthen it

1. _____

2. _____

3. _____

4. _____

5. _____

6. _____

7. _____

8. _____

9. _____

NAME _____ DATE _____

C-D WORDS IN CONTEXT 1

Now* learn some C-D *words that could* develop *your vocabulary very creatively.

Directions: Complete the sentences with words from the box. Hint: You will *not* use all the words. Check a dictionary if you need help.

cabaret

carbonated

civilian

cognizant

commuter

credence

custody

dahlia

defiance

depreciate

dexterity

disguise

dubious

1. Bob's silly _____ didn't fool anyone.

2. After 20 years in the army, Robert is now looking forward to _____ life.

3. Ginger's favorite _____ drink is ginger ale.

4. After reading the warning about jellyfish, I was _____ about going into the water.

5. Percy would rather go to a _____ than a regular restaurant because he enjoys the entertainment.

6. Samantha arranged a bouquet with irises, tulips, daffodils, and one perfect red _____.

7. Since Tim had always been so trustworthy, it was easy to put _____ in his unlikely story.

8. The willful child's _____ of the rules led to his expulsion from school.

9. The currency of that country continued to _____ for months.

10. The foster parents have had _____ of the child since December.

11. The juggler demonstrated great _____ when he juggled a bowling ball, a baseball, and a grapefruit.

12. The president was _____ of the situation, but he was powerless to do anything.

NAME _____ DATE _____

C-D WORDS IN CONTEXT 2

Directions: Read the definitions of the C-D words. Then use each word in an original sentence.

> **chafe** to make or become rough or sore by rubbing
>
> **chignon** a tight ball or roll of hair women wear at the back of the head
>
> **consequences** results or effects
>
> **correspond** to write or exchange letters
>
> **debtor** a person who owes something to another, such as money or services
>
> **dilemma** your position when faced with two poor choices
>
> **diversity** variety
>
> **dormant** asleep, or as if asleep
>
> **dwindle** to become steadily smaller or less; to shrink

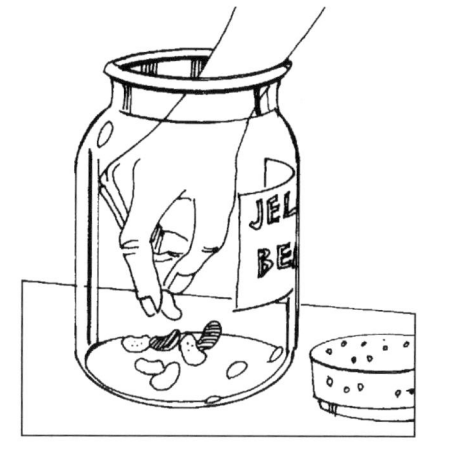

1. _____
2. _____
3. _____
4. _____
5. _____
6. _____
7. _____
8. _____
9. _____

NAME _____ DATE _____

E-F WORDS IN CONTEXT 1

Try adding some E-F words to your vocabulary to give it a little more élan and flair.

Directions: Complete the sentences with words from the box. Hint: You will *not* use all the words. Check a dictionary if you need help.

earnest

ecstasy

elaborate

emulate

escapade

exceed

fallible

fauna

firmament

flaunt

forfeit

forlorn

fragment

froth

1. Brandon's latest _____ resulted in two broken bones and a wrecked car.

2. Charles is often annoying, especially when he wants to _____ his knowledge of local history.

3. Flavio delivered a sincere and _____ apology to Misty.

4. If you _____ the speed limit, you are likely to get a traffic ticket.

5. Instead of using the word sky in her poem, Felicia used the word _____ to mean the same thing.

6. Don't believe everything Lester says, because, like all human beings, he is _____.

7. One _____ of the broken mirror remained hidden in the corner.

8. The _____ dinner Carmen prepared for her friends began with very tasty appetizers.

9. The _____ of that area includes deer, squirrels, bobcats, woodpeckers, and lizards.

10. When Clara blew out through the straw, a _____ formed on top of her root beer float.

11. You will be in _____ when you taste Chef Pierre's latest creation.

12. Young actors today often _____ the macho style of the young Marlon Brando.

NAME _____ DATE _____

E-F WORDS IN CONTEXT 2

Directions: Read the definitions of the E-F words. Then use each word in an original sentence.

ebullient bubbling over with high spirits and enthusiasm

edifice a building, especially a large and impressive structure

eloquence moving and skillful use of language, especially in speaking

equator an imaginary line that encircles the earth exactly halfway between the North Pole and the South Pole

estimate to make a close guess as to size, number, cost, etc.

exclude to keep out or shut out

faucet a device with an adjustable valve used to regulate the flow of a liquid, as from a pipe

fickle likely to change without warning; not constant in feeling, purpose, or nature

flamingo a pink or red wading bird that lives in tropical areas and has a long neck and long legs

flourish to grow vigorously; thrive

1. _____
2. _____
3. _____
4. _____
5. _____
6. _____
7. _____
8. _____
9. _____
10. _____

NAME _____   DATE _____

G-H WORDS IN CONTEXT 1

Learning some impressive **G-H** *words like* **grandiloquent** *can add some* **heft** *to your vocabulary.*

Directions: Complete the sentences with words from the box. Hint: You will *not* use all the words. Check a dictionary if you need help.

Word Box
gallant
garment
genuflect
goblet
grandiose
grimace
guilty
harvest
headquarters
hearth
heritage
homage
hypothetical

1. His dislocated shoulder caused Keith to _____ in pain.

2. I'd rather drink this beverage from a mug than from a _____.

3. In some churches, it is customary to _____ before entering a pew.

4. In the Middle Ages, vassals paid _____ to lords in exchange for protection.

5. Our town's police _____ is located at the corner of Fifth and Main.

6. Sylvia stored her fireplace tools on the raised _____ in the family room.

7. The furnishings in the _____ mansion were carved from the finest woods.

8. The _____ young man held the door open for his mother.

9. The _____ of the Irish includes fiddle music and dancing the jig.

10. We look forward to the fall _____ when all the apples ripen.

11. You'll enjoy wearing this _____ because it's made of the finest silk.

NAME _____ DATE _____

G-H WORDS IN CONTEXT 2

Directions: Read the definitions of the G-H words. Then use each word in an original sentence.

- **gallop** the fastest gait of a four-footed animal
- **gazpacho** a chilled soup made of tomatoes, spices, and other vegetables
- **glut** too great a supply of something
- **goulash** a stew of beef or veal with vegetables and paprika and other spices
- **gratifying** giving pleasure or satisfaction
- **haggle** to argue about the price of something
- **hazard** a dangerous or perilous situation
- **heap** a collection of things arranged in a pile
- **helmet** a protective covering for the head
- **hurdle** a small frame or fence to be jumped over in a race

1. _____
2. _____
3. _____
4. _____
5. _____
6. _____
7. _____
8. _____
9. _____
10. _____

NAME _____ DATE _____

I-J WORDS IN CONTEXT 1

You would be* imprudent, *or lacking in* judgment, *if you failed to add these* I-J *words to your vocabulary.

Directions: Complete the sentences with words from the box. Hint: You will *not* use all the words. Check a dictionary if you need help.

| identical | illusion | inconsistent | inexpensive | inhale | insomnia | itemize |
| jaguar | jargon | jiggle | jog | jumbo | jungle | juvenile |

1. A _____ is a large, spotted wild cat resembling a leopard.

2. A lush oasis is an optical _____ often seen in a desert.

3. Because these dresses are so _____, I think I'll buy several of them.

4. The door will open if you _____ the key in the lock a little bit.

5. Many types of animals are found only in the tropical _____.

6. Pedro couldn't finish the _____ ice cream cone before it started to melt.

7. The lawyers spoke in their own _____, making it difficult for anyone else to understand them.

8. The purses look _____, so how can I tell which one is a designer original?

9. The suspect's story was _____ from one day to the next.

10. This type of motion picture appeals mainly to a _____ audience.

11. When breathing, it's important to _____ deeply.

NAME _____ DATE _____

I-J WORDS IN CONTEXT 2

Directions: Read the definitions of the I-J words. Then use each word in an original sentence.

ideology the ideas or beliefs held by a class or group

inaugurate to install in an office with a formal ceremony

indigestion the inability to digest food, or difficulty in digesting food

infancy the time of being a baby

innovation a change in the usual way of doing things

janitor a person hired to clean and take care of a building

jest something said or done to provoke laughter; joke

jubilant joyful and proud

junction a point at which things meet or join

justice the quality of being fair and impartial

1. _____
2. _____
3. _____
4. _____
5. _____
6. _____
7. _____
8. _____
9. _____
10. _____

NAME _____ DATE _____

K-L WORDS IN CONTEXT 1

It's not all that laborious *to add to your* knowledge *of* K-L *words, so let's* look *at a few.*

Directions: Complete the sentences with words from the box. Hint: You will *not* use all the words. Check a dictionary if you need help.

Word Box
kaleidoscope
keg
kernel
kindle
kiosk
kosher
lacquer
languid
ledge
leisure
lenient
literacy
lopsided

1. A child's first step toward achieving _____ is learning the alphabet.

2. We need every _____ of corn from these cobs to make the corn chowder.

3. In Patrick's _____ time, he likes to do crossword puzzles.

4. Mr. Porter buys his morning newspaper at the _____ on the corner.

5. Once we applied _____ to the table, it was as shiny as the rest of the furniture.

6. The beginner made a vase in her ceramics class, but it turned out a bit _____.

7. The ever-changing patterns made by a _____ became the subject of the artist's paintings.

8. The hot weather had us all feeling quite _____ and slightly grumpy.

9. The only kind of pickles Tom will eat are _____ dills.

10. This wooden _____ holds 10 gallons of apple cider.

11. We have to _____ these small pieces of wood to get the campfire started.

NAME _____ DATE _____

K-L WORDS IN CONTEXT 2

Directions: Read the definitions of the K-L words. Then use each word in an original sentence.

- **kangaroo** an Australian animal, the female of which carries the young in a pouch
- **kelp** a coarse, brown seaweed
- **keyboard** the row or rows of keys, as in a piano or a computer
- **kinship** relationship, especially by blood
- **kumquat** a sour, tangy citrus fruit resembling a tiny orange
- **landmark** a hill, tree, etc. used to recognize a place
- **ledge** a shelf, sill, or other surface jutting out from a wall or window
- **liquefy** to make or become liquid
- **loiter** to linger or dawdle
- **luxury** anything costly but unnecessary that gives comfort or pleasure, but is not necessary to life or health

1. _____
2. _____
3. _____
4. _____
5. _____
6. _____
7. _____
8. _____
9. _____
10. _____

© Saddleback Educational Publishing • www.sdlback.com
Common Core Skills & Strategies for Vocabulary: Level 7
CCSS: L.7.4, L.7.4a, L.7.4b, L.7.4c, L.7.4d, L.7.6, W.7.4

NAME _____   DATE _____

M-N WORDS IN CONTEXT 1

Don't neglect *these* M-N *words. If you study them well, you'll remove all* mystery *about their meanings.*

Directions: Complete the sentences with words from the box. Hint: You will *not* use all the words. Check a dictionary if you need help.

mahogany	martyr	menace	mildew	modem	mortality	muffin
naive	necessary	nobility	nomadic	nonchalant	nozzle	nudge

1. A _____ is someone who will suffer or die rather than give up his or her beliefs.

2. As a member of a _____ tribe, Ahmed moved constantly in search of food.

3. Beatrice is _____ if she believes every salesperson's claims.

4. Dominick needs to get a _____ so he can hook up to the Internet.

5. Grace usually has a blueberry _____ and some tea for breakfast.

6. Isabel gave Clara a little _____ to get her attention.

7. Keith needs to replace the _____ on his garden hose.

8. _____ developed in the damp closet, ruining many of Maxine's clothes.

9. Sadie couldn't decide between teak and _____ for her new furniture.

10. That vicious criminal is a _____ to society!

11. The crowd was excited, but the quarterback seemed almost _____ about the victory.

12. Your help on this project is absolutely _____ to our success.

NAME _____ DATE _____

M-N WORDS IN CONTEXT 2

Directions: Read the definitions of the M-N words. Then use each word in an original sentence.

macaroni hollow pasta tubes often baked with cheese
manipulate to operate or work with the hands; handle
matriarch female ruler or head, as of her family, tribe, or community
miser a greedy, stingy person who hoards money instead of using it
mysterious impossible or difficult to explain or understand
navigation the art of charting the position and course of a ship or aircraft
neutral not on one side or the other in a dispute, contest, or war
notify to give notice to; to inform

nourish to keep alive and healthy by feeding
nugget a lump, especially of gold in its natural state

1. _____
2. _____
3. _____
4. _____
5. _____
6. _____
7. _____
8. _____
9. _____
10. _____

NAME _____ DATE _____

O-P WORDS IN CONTEXT 1

You can't be overly prepared *for vocabulary tests. So add these* O-P words *to your list.*

Directions: Complete the sentences with words from the box. Hint: You will *not* use all the words. Check a dictionary if you need help.

obituary	octave	omnivorous	ordeal	original
ottoman	overalls	pagan	patriarch	pedicure
phantom	plateau	posture	prize	purpose

1. Aaron stands up so straight he could be a model for good _____.

2. As _____ of the family, Murray was responsible for 14 people.

3. Carla sang the song a full _____ higher than James did.

4. Gloria chooses a different nail polish color every time she gets a _____.

5. By nature humans are _____ creatures, but some people prefer to be herbivorous.

6. Jessica's _____ began when she got lost in the forest.

7. Ms. Jefferson's _____ said that she had lived for 93 years.

8. Although it was an accident, Sherri thought Colleen had tripped her on _____.

9. That brown _____ does not look right with the black chair.

10. The _____ for best apple pie went to Amos this year.

11. The scary story told of a _____ ship that seemed to appear every December.

12. You need the _____ sales receipt to return something to the store.

NAME _____ DATE _____

O-P WORDS IN CONTEXT 2

Directions: Read the definitions of the O-P words. Then use each word in an original sentence.

obscurity the condition of being hidden or unknown

official a person who holds an office or position, as in the government or a business

opposition the act of being against something; resistance

outskirts the outer edges or areas far from the center, as of a city

oxygen a colorless, tasteless, odorless gaseous element making up about a fifth of the earth's atmosphere

parka a fur or cloth jacket, or a coat with a hood

pillar a slender, firm, upright structure of stone, wood, or other material

plunder to rob of goods or property by force; to loot

prescription a physician's formula for preparing and ordering a medicine

prowl to roam about quietly and slyly, as in search of food or something to steal

1. _____
2. _____
3. _____
4. _____
5. _____
6. _____
7. _____
8. _____
9. _____
10. _____

NAME _____ DATE _____

Q-R WORDS IN CONTEXT 1

Quick! Run! *Let's hurry to learn these* Q-R *words.*

Directions: Complete the sentences with words from the box. Hint: You will *not* use all the words. Check a dictionary if you need help.

quad	quake	queasy	quell	quince
quite	quota	rampage	redeem	repent
reverse	rote	rouse	rupture	

1. Did the criminal ever _____ for the suffering he caused that family?

2. Gladys makes jelly from the fruit of the _____ tree in her yard.

3. If the rebels don't stop their activities, the government will move in to _____ the revolt.

4. At lunchtime, Mickey met Jean in the center of the _____.

5. Sally plans to _____ her coupons for a new toaster oven.

6. The club met its _____ of magazine sales.

7. When it was left alone too long, the dog went on a _____ in the yard.

8. The _____ lasted only 30 seconds, but it did tremendous damage.

9. There's a picture of a building on the _____ side of that coin.

10. Sam feels a little _____ whenever he reads in a moving car.

11. That awful smell was caused by a _____ in a gas line.

NAME _____ DATE _____

Q-R WORDS IN CONTEXT 2

Directions: Read the definitions of the Q–R words. Then use each word in an original sentence.

quarantine the isolation of persons exposed to contagious diseases

quart a measure of liquid volume equal to 32 ounces, two pints, or 1/4 gallon

quaver to tremble or shake in an uncertain way, as a voice

quiz a short or informal test given to a student or students

quotient the number that results if one number is divided by another

radius a straight line from the center of a circle or sphere to the circumference or surface

reap to cut down or gather in (grain); harvest (a crop)

regret to feel sorrow or grief about something

resist to work or strive against; oppose

ripple to form into small waves

1. _____
2. _____
3. _____
4. _____
5. _____
6. _____
7. _____
8. _____
9. _____
10. _____

NAME _____ DATE _____

S-T WORDS IN CONTEXT 1

Do you have the* temerity *to learn and use these* S-T *words in your everyday vocabulary? If so, that's just* swell!

Directions: Complete the sentences with words from the box. Hint: You will *not* use all the words. Check a dictionary if you need help.

Word Box
sacrifice
segment
silhouette
smear
spare
stiff
swelter
tactful
temerity
temper
thorn
tortoise
triceps
tyranny

1. After taking assertiveness lessons, Jake finally had the _____ to ask for a raise.

2. It wasn't very _____ to ask June about the breakup with her boyfriend.

3. Dennis was developing his _____ by working out at the gym.

4. Giving up dessert for a month was a great _____ for Gina.

5. You will _____ the paint if you touch it before it dries.

6. Marlene's painfully _____ neck prevented her from driving.

7. Mr. Chavez has been in a good _____ since his business improved.

8. Alex carefully cut out a _____ of Abraham Lincoln.

9. The record-breaking heat caused all of us to _____ the entire weekend.

10. The _____ tire came in very handy when we had a flat.

11. There's a particularly large _____ on the stem of this rose.

12. Walter eagerly watched the third _____ of the five-part series.

NAME _____ DATE _____

S-T WORDS IN CONTEXT 2

Directions: Read the definitions of the S-T words. Then use each word in an original sentence.

---

scheme a plan or plot, especially one that's secret and sly
shield to protect or guard
squadron in the U.S. Navy, a group or unit of vessels or aircraft
subtle not direct or obvious; hard to see or understand
syrup a thick, sweet liquid, as that made by boiling sugar with a liquid
tantalize to tease by offering something and then holding it back
thirst dryness in the mouth and throat caused by a need to drink
tithe a tax or offering of 10 percent of one's income to support a church
transform to greatly change the form or appearance of
tusk a long, pointed, projecting tooth, generally one of a pair, as in the elephant

---

1. _____
2. _____
3. _____
4. _____
5. _____
6. _____
7. _____
8. _____
9. _____
10. _____

NAME _____ DATE _____

U-V WORDS IN CONTEXT 1

Exercise your vocal cords by utilizing these U-V words in your oral vocabulary.

Directions: Complete the sentences with words from the box. Hint: You will *not* use all the words. Check a dictionary if you need help.

Word Box
ulcer
unaccompanied
undisciplined
unkempt
unsound
uptown
utter
valid
varnish
venture
vestment
vicinity
vivid
vulgar

1. After stripping and sanding the floors, we applied a clear _____.

2. An _____ minor must be met by someone after a flight.

3. Despite her mother's efforts to keep her clean, Monica always seemed _____.

4. Marsha suffers from a very painful stomach _____.

5. Pamela makes a poor impression because she wears _____ clothing styles.

6. Robert has a _____ imagination, which is useful in his career as a writer.

7. The _____ puppy was making life miserable for the fussy family.

8. Her restaurant is located in the _____ of the downtown park.

9. Felicia's _____ plan has no chance of succeeding.

10. This coupon is _____ only until August 15.

11. When our flashlights failed, we were surrounded by _____ darkness.

NAME _____ DATE _____

U-V WORDS IN CONTEXT 2

Directions: Read the definitions of the U-V words. Then use each word in an original sentence.

- **umiak** a large, open Native Alaskan boat, made of skins drawn over a wooden frame
- **undefeated** not defeated or conquered
- **ungrateful** lacking gratitude; not thankful
- **unpopular** not liked or approved of by a rather large number of people
- **untidy** not orderly or neat; messy
- **vandal** person who is willfully destructive
- **velocity** rate of motion or speed
- **verify** to prove to be true or accurate; to confirm
- **vim** force or vigor; energy; spirit
- **violence** force used to cause injury or damage

1. _____
2. _____
3. _____
4. _____
5. _____
6. _____
7. _____
8. _____
9. _____
10. _____

NAME _____ DATE _____

W-X WORDS IN CONTEXT 1

You don't need X-ray *vision to see how* worthwhile *it would be to add these* W-X *words to your vocabulary.*

Directions: Complete the sentences with words from the box. Hint: You will *not* use all the words. Check a dictionary if you need help.

wad	wade	wallet	warble	waylay	wharf
whiff	X-axis	xenophobe	xerography	xerothermic	xylem

1. As Wendy walked past the jasmine blossoms, she got a _____ of their aroma.

2. Dorian labeled the _____ on her graph, using very neat numbers.

3. Few plants were able to survive during that _____ period.

4. It's too bad that Oscar is a _____, because he misses out on some interesting friendships.

5. Jan enjoyed going down to the _____ to eat lunch by the bay.

6. Lottie always liked to keep a small _____ of cash tucked away in her purse.

7. The water was shallow enough for us to _____ to the other side.

8. _____ is found in the stems or trunk of a plant.

9. This machine uses the process of _____ to make photocopies.

10. Vic forgot his _____, so his friend had to pay for his dinner.

11. We were awakened each morning by the _____ of a lovely bird.

108 CCSS: L.7.4, L.7.4a, L.7.4b, L.7.4c, L.7.4d, L.7.6, W.7.4

Common Core Skills & Strategies for Vocabulary: Level 7

NAME _____   DATE _____

W-X WORDS IN CONTEXT 2

Directions: Read the definitions of the W-X words. Then use each word in an original sentence.

wafer a thin, crisp biscuit
wasteland a barren, desolate area
weld joining (pieces of metal) by heating or pressing
whimper to cry with low, mournful, broken sounds
wreath a woven ring of flowers or leaves
xanthic yellow or yellowish
xebec a small, three-masted vessel, once used by Algerian pirates in the Mediterranean Sea
xeric having to do with or adapted to a very dry environment
xeriscape a landscape design that relies on little or no water
xerophyte a plant adapted to growing and surviving in a dry environment

1. _____
2. _____
3. _____
4. _____
5. _____
6. _____
7. _____
8. _____
9. _____
10. _____

NAME _____   DATE _____

Y-Z WORDS IN CONTEXT 1

You don't have to be a word* zealot *to say* yes *to learning these* Y-Z *words.

Directions: Complete the sentences with words from the box. Hint: You will *not* use all the words. Check a dictionary if you need help.

yacht
yam
yearling
yelp
yoga
yogurt
youth
zealot
zenith
zeppelin
zinnia
zodiac
zori

1. Bruce often has _____ and granola for breakfast.

2. The _____ has lived at the animal preserve since its birth.

3. Gwyneth rolled up her _____ mat after the 4:00 class concluded.

4. Marvin wants to buy a _____ when he earns his first million.

5. Olivia would rather have a _____ than a baked potato.

6. The signs of the _____ are used in the practice of astrology.

7. The wild-eyed _____ tried to convince us to read his book.

8. When Martha tripped over the dog, the poor animal let out a loud _____.

9. During her final worldwide tour, the singer was at the _____ of her popularity.

10. After the strap on her _____ broke, Shirley's foot burned on the hot sand.

11. Zeke's _____ garden is the most colorful flower garden on the block.

NAME _____ DATE _____

Y-Z WORDS IN CONTEXT 2

Directions: Read the definitions of the Y-Z words. Then use each word in an original sentence.

yahoo a brutish or crude person

yawn to open the mouth wide with a long intake of breath, as when sleepy or bored

yeast a substance used in bread-making that allows the dough to rise

yodel to sing in the form of a warble, with rapid voice changes from normal to a shrill falsetto

yoke a curved, wooden frame that joins two animals, such as oxen

zeal great interest and devotion; enthusiasm

zebra a striped animal related to the horse

zephyr any soft, gentle wind

zest keen enjoyment; great pleasure

zoom to move with a low-pitched but loud humming sound

1. _____
2. _____
3. _____
4. _____
5. _____
6. _____
7. _____
8. _____
9. _____
10. _____

NAME _____   DATE _____

JUST FOR FUN: EXPLAINING WHY OR WHY NOT

Have some fun with these questions that explore your knowledge of some interesting words.

Directions: Check a dictionary to help you answer the questions.

1. Why would a **fakir** be unlikely to wear a **fedora**?
   _____
   _____

2. Would it be easier to study the moon at its **perigee** or at its **apogee**? Why?
   _____
   _____

3. Why would it amaze everyone to see an **ascetic** attired in **silk**?
   _____
   _____

4. Why would it not be surprising to see a **buccaneer** on a **brigantine**?
   _____
   _____

5. Why would an **impostor** travel **incognito**?
   _____
   _____

6. Would you rather have a necklace of **lodestones** or **rhinestones**? Why?
   _____
   _____

7. Why would a railroad worker be more likely to use a **semaphore** than a **metaphor**? Why?
   _____
   _____

8. Would you be more likely to ride a **jennet** or a **jenny**? Why?
   _____
   _____

JUST FOR FUN: EXPLORING BIG WORDS

Have some fun with big words as you build your vocabulary.

Directions: Check the dictionary definitions of the **boldface** words to help you answer the questions.

1. Would a teacher be more likely to use **legerdemain** or a **lectern**? Explain your answer. _____
_____
_____

2. Would you rather be regarded as someone full of **rectitude** or **iniquity**? Why?
_____
_____
_____

3. Would it be more dangerous to spend time with a **bellicose** person or a **comatose** person? Explain your answer. _____
_____

4. Whom would you rather have as a friend—a **loquacious** person or a **mendacious** person? Why? _____
_____

5. What would make more sense for a recovering patient—a **reversible** bed or an **adjustable** bed? Why? _____
_____

6. Would you be more likely to see a **bobolink** in a **metropolitan** or agrarian setting? Why? _____
_____

7. If you were an employer, would you rather hire someone who had **versatility** or someone who had **culpability**? Explain your answer. _____
_____

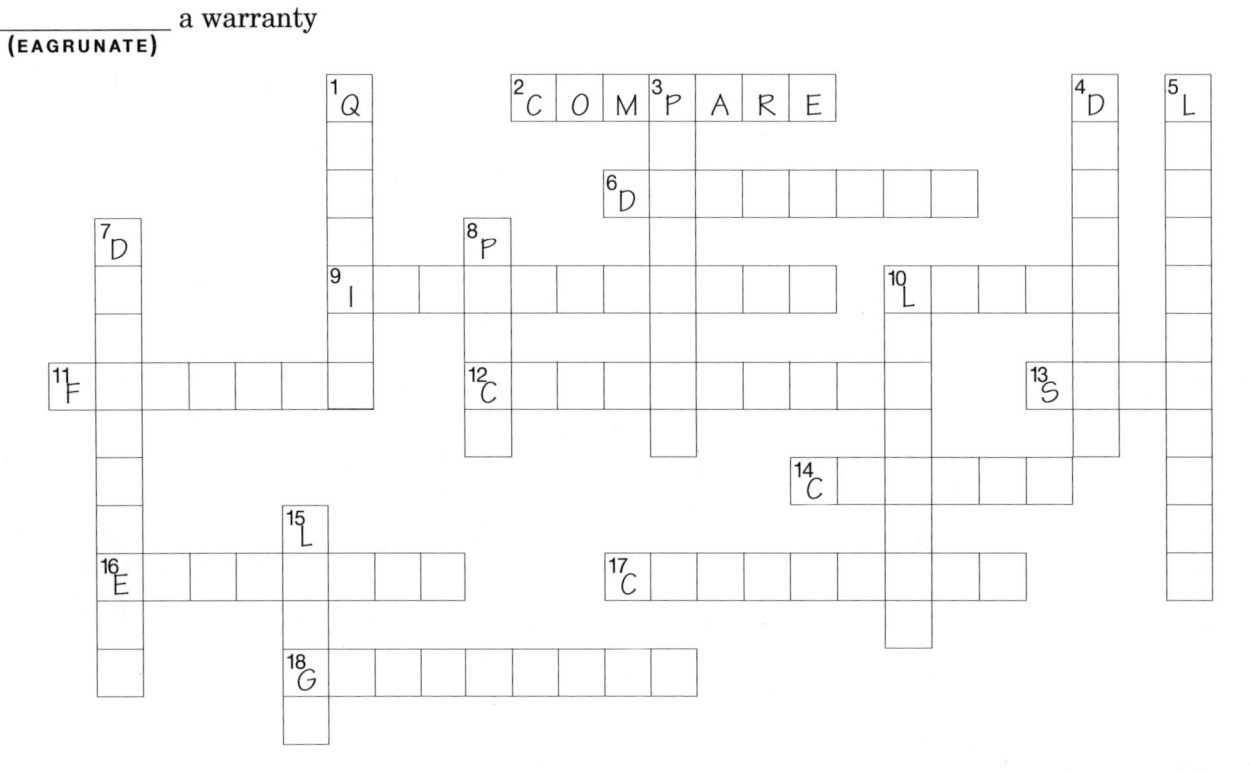

NAME _____   DATE _____

SHOPPING WORDS 1

Directions: Unscramble the words that match the definitions. Then use the unscrambled words to complete the crossword puzzle. Item 2-Across has been done for you.

ACROSS

2. __compare__ (MACEROP) what you do with prices
6. _____ (CINDOSUT) an amount taken off the usual price
9. _____ (GREDINTINES) what's listed on a food label
10. _____ (BALEL) a tag on the inside of clothing
11. _____ (CRAYTOF) place where things are manufactured
12. _____ (PASOCRONIM) a smart kind of shopping
13. _____ (LESA) a special event in a store
14. _____ (TICERD) one way to pay for things
16. _____ (HAXENCEG) what to do if something doesn't fit
17. _____ (SMECICOTS) the department in a store where you buy lipsticks
18. _____ (EAGRUNATE) a warranty

DOWN

1. _____ (YALQUIT) what you look for in clothing
3. _____ (GACITPER) where you look for the cost of an item
4. _____ (RYD NEALC) an instruction for cleaning clothes (2 words)
5. _____ (THIGWLEGITH) feature you'd want in summer clothing
7. _____ (TEDPTARMNE) a section in a store
8. _____ (CEPRI) the cost to the customer
10. _____ (EGELIRNI) the department where you'd buy a nightgown
15. _____ (GERLA) the size for a big person

114 CCSS: L.7.2b, L.7.4, L.7.4a, L.7.5, L.7.5b, RH.6-8.4, RST.6-8.4

NAME _____ DATE _____

SHOPPING WORDS 2

Directions: Use the crossword puzzle answers to correctly complete the sentences.

1. Be sure to buy all the _____ you need to make a special meal; make sure you get everything you need.

2. Mabel buys all her clothing at the _____ outlet stores.

3. So the _____ won't show through, you might have to cut it out of a sheer shirt.

4. This _____ store sells clothing, household goods, cosmetics, and shoes.

5. It can be expensive to take care of clothes whose care instructions say, "_____ only."

6. You can often get a _____ on clothing that is out of season.

7. Doris gave her friend a gift receipt so she could _____ the gift if she didn't like it.

8. Clothing that is of poor _____ never lasts very long.

9. Patrick bought his mom some perfume at the _____ counter.

10. If you shop with a _____ card, you don't have to carry a lot of cash with you.

11. The _____ showed that the _____ had been marked down three times.

12. James bought his athletic shoes on _____ for 25 percent off.

© Saddleback Educational Publishing • www.sdlback.com
Common Core Skills & Strategies for Vocabulary: Level 7
CCSS: L.7.2b, L.7.4, L.7.4a, L.7.5, L.7.5b, RH.6-8.4, RST.6-8.4   115

NAME _____   DATE _____

LAW WORDS 1

Directions: Unscramble the words that match the definitions. Then use the unscrambled words to complete the crossword puzzle. Item 2-Across has been done for you.

ACROSS

2. __swear__ (RESAW) what you do when you take an oath
6. _____ (RYJU) the people who decide guilt or innocence
7. _____ (STIFYET) what witnesses do on the stand
9. _____ (RALPOE) to release a prisoner early under certain conditions
10. _____ (ENECSTEN) what the judge determines
11. _____ (LATIR) the process of hearing a case in court
14. _____ (MASTIUMON) a lawyer's closing argument
15. _____ (TANDFEEDN) person accused of a crime
16. _____ (HTURT) what witnesses are required to tell
17. _____ (GAURE) what lawyers do in court
18. _____ (FEEDENS) the team that protects the accused

DOWN

1. _____ (TINPILFAF) another name for the accuser
3. _____ (SETWINS) a person called to testify
4. _____ (ONIBATRPO) a possible sentence for a minor first-time offense
5. _____ (ISOCRETPUNO) the legal team that makes the accusation
6. _____ (TECJUIS) what the legal system strives to achieve
8. _____ (DIRVECT) what the jury arrives at in the jury room
12. _____ (TAOTRENY) another word for lawyer
13. _____ (DEJUG) person in charge in the courtroom

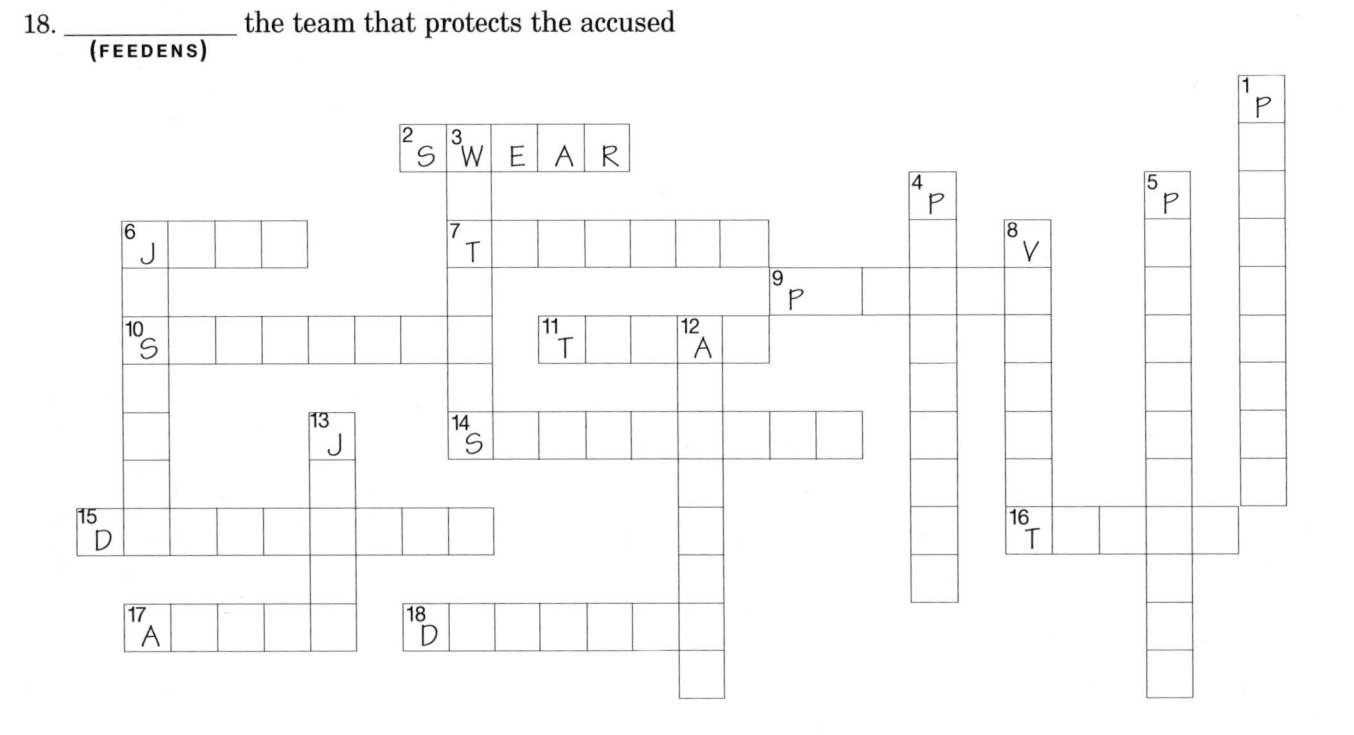

NAME _____   DATE _____

LAW WORDS 2

Directions: Use the crossword puzzle answers to correctly complete the sentences. You will use one word twice.

1. Every _____ must take an oath before taking the stand.

2. The teenager got six months' _____ for his minor offense.

3. The _____ of innocence was quite a surprise to everyone in the courtroom.

4. Every accused person is entitled to a fair _____.

5. A _____ of one's peers listens to the arguments made in court.

6. The lawyer for the _____ accused the young woman of stealing.

7. The newspaper reports showed sympathy for the _____, who had never been accused of anything before.

8. The _____ attorney claimed that his client had an airtight alibi.

9. The _____ called in a series of expert witnesses to back up the plaintiff's claim.

10. The witness had to swear to tell the _____.

11. The _____ wore a black robe and a serious expression.

12. The upset family of the convicted man said that _____ had not been served.

NAME _____   DATE _____

BUILDING WORDS 1

Directions: Unscramble the words that match the definitions. Then use the unscrambled words to complete the crossword puzzle. Item 1-Across has been done for you.

ACROSS

1. __permits__ (PITREMS) licenses the city issues to approve building plans
5. _____ (DAGSLIPNACN) vegetation on the grounds around a building
6. _____ (ORNIGARITI) system installed to carry water to plants
10. _____ (LOREBULDZ) a piece of heavy equipment that moves dirt
11. _____ (TINUCTROSCON) another word for the act of building
12. _____ (YADWLRL) what covers a wall's framework on the inside
14. _____ (UTIFADONON) the basis of any building
15. _____ (CHATTERIC) the person who draws up plans for a building

DOWN

2. _____ (NIGSLEHS) possible covering for a roof
3. _____ (TOPIA) a concrete area, usually in the backyard
4. _____ (CETERILICNA) the worker who installs wiring
7. _____ (LRPEUMB) the worker who installs pipes
8. _____ (CRECTONE) a liquid material that gradually becomes very hard
9. _____ (NORCROCTAT) an independent worker who agrees to do a job
13. _____ (LUBRENPIT) the drawn plan for a building

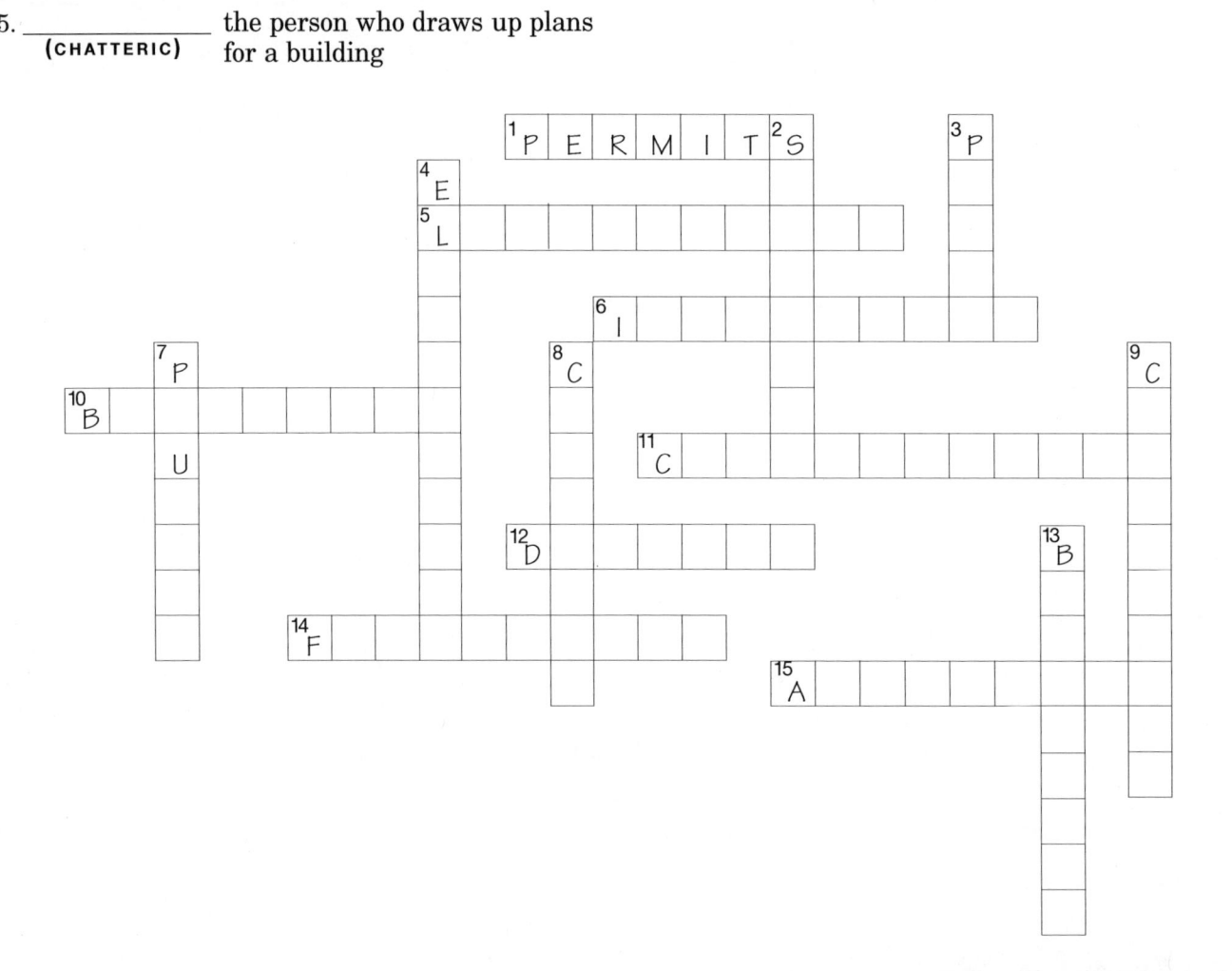

118   CCSS: L.7.2b, L.7.4, L.7.4a, L.7.5, L.7.5b, RH.6-8.4, RST.6-8.4

NAME _____ DATE _____

BUILDING WORDS 2

Directions: Use the crossword puzzle answers to correctly complete the sentences.

1. Once the basic _____ was in place, Helen added her favorite flowers here and there.

2. The _____ system in the yard consisted of 16 sprinklers and some drip hoses.

3. For the roof covering, George preferred _____ rather than tiles.

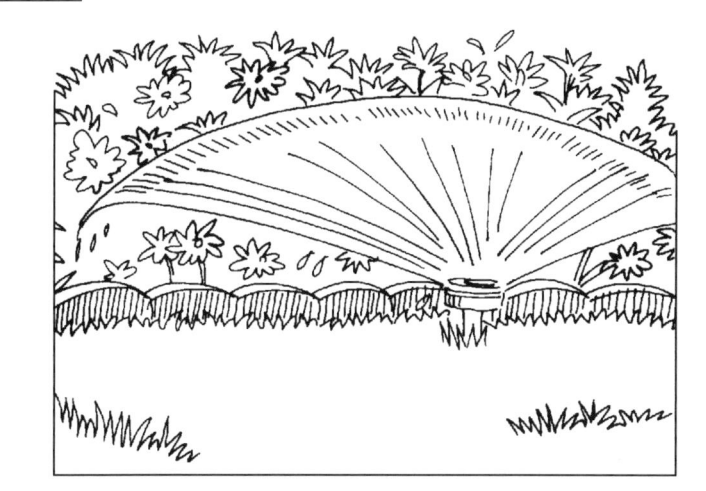

4. The general contractor referred to the _____ to see what the architect intended.

5. The _____ who drew up the plan is well-known in the city for his innovative designs.

6. The Johnsons enjoyed eating dinner on their new _____ in the backyard.

7. The _____ installed new pipes and fixtures in the bathroom and kitchen.

8. Because of zoning restrictions, the city was reluctant to issue _____ for an extra unit.

9. The _____ in the driveway had been stamped to look like cobblestones.

10. The _____ recommended installing lights under the kitchen cabinets.

11. _____ of the new home began in October and was completed in May.

12. The general _____ for the project hired people he had worked with before.

© Saddleback Educational Publishing • www.sdlback.com
Common Core Skills & Strategies for Vocabulary: Level 7   CCSS: L.7.2b, L.7.4, L.7.4a, L.7.5, L.7.5b, RH.6-8.4, RST.6-8.4   **119**

NAME _____   DATE _____

SPACE WORDS 1

Directions: Unscramble the words that match the definitions. Then use the unscrambled words to complete the crossword puzzle. Item 2-Across has been done for you.

ACROSS

2. __propulsion__ a force that causes forward movement
   (PINPURSOLO)
6. _____ a jet-propelled device that shoots through the air
   (CERTOK)
7. _____ between or among the stars
   (TENLIRTALERS)
8. _____ a person who travels in space
   (SORANTATU)
9. _____ the path taken by a celestial body or artificial satellite around its center of attraction
   (BOIRT)
10. _____ to hurl or fling into space
    (NUCLAH)
12. _____ something considered endless and without limits, such as space or time
    (TINYINIF)
14. _____ the natural satellite of Earth
    (ONMO)
16. _____ a celestial body that revolves around a larger celestial body
    (LESALITTE)
17. _____ six types of particles thought to be basic units of matter
    (RAQUKS)

DOWN

1. _____ a vehicle, such as a rocket or artificial satellite, designed for travel in outer space
   (SCRTPEFACA)
3. _____ between or among planets
   (RPIYRNATTENELA)
4. _____ a large system of celestial bodies
   (LAYGAX)
5. _____ a force that draws bodies in the earth's sphere toward the center of the earth
   (VIGATRY)
11. _____ the universe as a complete and harmonious system
    (MOCOSS)
13. _____ any of the relatively large, non-glowing bodies that move in orbits around the sun
    (PELTAN)
15. _____ a celestial body that sends pulses of radio waves at rapid, regular intervals
    (LAPRUS)

120 CCSS: L.7.2b, L.7.4, L.7.4a, L.7.5, L.7.5b, RH.6-8.4, RST.6-8.4

NAME _____ DATE _____

SPACE WORDS 2

Directions: Use the crossword puzzle answers to correctly complete the sentences.

1. Sally Ride was the first female American _____ to go into space.

2. A _____ is used to propel fireworks, missiles, and space vehicles.

3. NASA plans to _____ another rocket in about three months.

4. The weather satellite is now in _____ around Earth.

5. Once a spaceship enters the atmosphere, the force of _____ pulls it toward Earth.

6. Earth is part of a _____ called the Milky Way.

7. Jupiter is the largest _____ in our solar system.

8. Our _____ revolves around the earth but does not rotate on an axis.

9. Because of the great distances between stars, _____ travel would take light years.

10. _____ travel seems within the reach of science in the relatively near future.

11. Scientists record the radio waves sent by the distant _____.

12. No scientist has ever actually seen a _____.

© Saddleback Educational Publishing • www.sdlback.com
Common Core Skills & Strategies for Vocabulary: Level 7   CCSS: L.7.2b, L.7.4, L.7.4a, L.7.5, L.7.5b, RH.6-8.4, RST.6-8.4   121

NAME _____   DATE _____

HEALTH WORDS 1

Directions: Unscramble the words that match the definitions. Then use the unscrambled words to complete the crossword puzzle. Item 4-Across has been done for you.

ACROSS

4. __muscular__ (SMUURLAC) — This type of person is very strong.
6. _____ (STESRS) — emotional or mental strain or tension
9. _____ (NITAVMI) — an organic substance found in most natural foods and needed for good health
10. _____ (PILCRALAY) — any of the narrow, threadlike blood vessels connecting arteries with veins
13. _____ (BEFRI) — coarse food parts that stimulate the movement of food through the intestines
14. _____ (PILDI) — any of a group of organic compounds including fats, oils, and waxes
15. _____ (MANTERTET) — what you need if you get sick
16. _____ (BEHRAETAT) — what a doctor listens for with a stethoscope

DOWN

1. _____ (LACIVCADSROAUR) — relating to the health of your heart and blood vessels
2. _____ (NORNIUITT) — food; nourishment
3. _____ (SNIMIONA) — difficulty in sleeping; sleeplessness
4. _____ (NELIRMA) — a natural substance necessary to the human diet
5. _____ (DATCYAHROBRES) — starches such as rice, potatoes, pasta, bread
7. _____ (TUAGFIE) — a weary condition resulting from hard work, effort, or strain
8. _____ (TIMELOMABS) — the rate at which your body burns calories
11. _____ (TCSERTH) — what you need to do before exercising to avoid injury
12. _____ (MOSTYPM) — a sign of an illness

NAME _____ DATE _____

HEALTH WORDS 2

Directions: Use the crossword puzzle answers to correctly complete the sentences.

1. Gene takes a _____ pill the first thing each morning.

2. Foods that are good for quick energy before a race are _____.

3. Because she works out regularly, Gretchen has a very _____ body.

4. Good _____, proper rest, and adequate exercise are necessary for good health.

5. Before and after his workouts, Timothy likes to slowly _____ his muscles.

6. During aerobic exercise, you should raise your _____ for at least 20 minutes.

7. Edward is under a great deal of _____ at work, which is making him ill.

8. One way to build strong muscles is to work them to _____ and then rest.

9. You might be able to cure _____ by getting plenty of exercise during the day.

10. The first _____ of a cold might be a scratchy throat.

11. The more muscular you are, the higher your rate of _____ will be.

12. The best _____ for a cold is rest and plenty of liquids.

NAME _____   DATE _____

BUSINESS WORDS 1

Directions: Unscramble the words that match the definitions. Then use the unscrambled words to complete the crossword puzzle. Item 1-Across has been done for you.

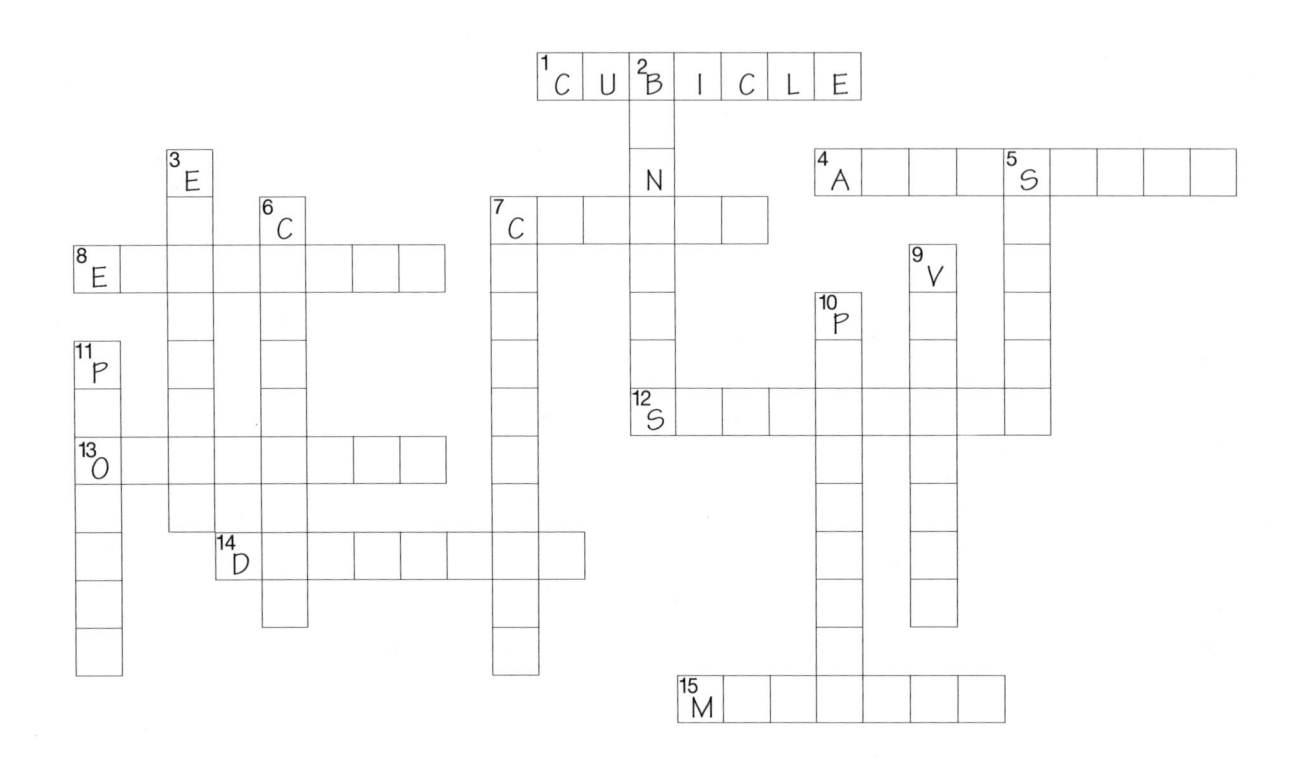

ACROSS

1. _cubicle_ a small work enclosure
   (ECICBUL)
4. _____ one who helps another
   (SIATSANST)
7. _____ a customer
   (LECTIN)
8. _____ a paid worker
   (EPEYMOLE)
12. _____ one who writes letters and performs other administrative duties
    (RESARCETY)
13. _____ work beyond 40 hours
    (MEROTIVE)
14. _____ the date something is due
    (EDILEDAN)
15. _____ a gathering
    (MINETEG)

DOWN

2. _____ things employees get in addition to their regular pay, such as insurance, vacation pay, sick pay
   (FEBIENTS)
3. _____ one who hires others
   (MYRELOPE)
5. _____ a worker's pay
   (ASRAYL)
6. _____ a group of people working together
   (MITECOTME)
7. _____ a meeting at which a discussion is held
   (FENECEORNC)
9. _____ time off from work
   (NOCAVIAT)
10. _____ the head of a company
    (SIPERNTED)
11. _____ an assignment
    (JCTPORE)

BUSINESS WORDS 2

Directions: Use the crossword puzzle answers to correctly complete the sentences.

1. When she took her _____, Brenda went fly-fishing in Montana.

2. The _____ requested that his parts be manufactured in three months.

3. Mark, Joel, Katie, and Julia are on the _____ to plan the company picnic.

4. As an _____ of this company, you are expected to get to work by nine o'clock.

5. This is a huge _____, and we'll need everyone's cooperation to finish it.

6. The _____ for the new project is July 18.

7. The ad claimed, "We are an equal-opportunity _____."

8. The _____ at this company include a yearly two-week paid vacation and 10 paid sick days.

9. Diane's _____ was 10 percent higher than it had been at her previous job.

10. Pete gets paid time-and-a-half for working _____.

11. As Alicia's _____, Tyrone is responsible for all of her clerical work.

12. Jacob is the _____ and chief executive officer of his own company.

NAME _____   DATE _____

TRAVEL WORDS 1

Directions: Unscramble the words that match the definitions. Then use the unscrambled words to complete the crossword puzzle. Item 1-Across has been done for you.

ACROSS

1. _tropical_ (PORTCLAI) — the climate in Hawaii
3. _____ (ISARAF) — a popular tourist activity in Africa
4. _____ (SAPOPRST) — the type of identification you need to travel internationally
7. _____ (TENRURASAT) — a place to eat when you're on vacation
9. _____ (OMAMTIDACOONCS) — lodgings; room and board
12. _____ (THEOL) — a place to sleep when you're on vacation
13. _____ (IGNIGSTHESE) — the kind of trips tourists often like to take
15. _____ (DRAPMIYS) — a popular tourist attraction in Egypt
16. _____ (VUISEONR) — what a tourist likes to buy
17. _____ (LATANRSET) — what you must do to understand a foreign language

DOWN

2. _____ (FARRIAE) — what it costs to fly on a plane
3. _____ (CUASIETS) — what you carry your clothes in
5. _____ (TISNAPTROTRANO) — planes, trains, and taxis, for example
6. _____ (TYCUSREI) — a checkpoint where luggage is examined for safety
8. _____ (HHOTPAGORPS) — what tourists like to take with cameras
10. _____ (UMSEMU) — a place to see a country's artworks
11. _____ (UDGIE) — a person who might take you around, pointing out the sights
14. _____ (TOITRUS) — a person who visits another city or country

[Crossword grid with 1-Across filled in as "TROPICAL"]

126 CCSS: L.7.2b, L.7.4, L.7.4a, L.7.5, L.7.5b, RH.6-8.4, RST.6-8.4

NAME _____ DATE _____

TRAVEL WORDS 2

Directions: Use the crossword puzzle answers to correctly complete the sentences.

1. The _____ are the ancient burial places of Egyptian pharaohs.

2. While on vacation Jenny's favorite means of _____ is a bicycle.

3. Mona's _____ picture is unusually good.

4. At the _____ checkpoint, Martha had to take off her shoes and her jacket.

5. The _____ on that airline includes a meal and a movie.

6. Jed had to buy a bigger _____ so he could pack enough clothes for his trip.

7. Marianne's _____ room was a large one overlooking Central Park.

8. Ted's _____ plans included a visit to the Lincoln Memorial.

9. Victoria speaks French, so she can _____ for Dan when they're in Paris.

10. The only _____ Hank bought in Mexico was a sombrero.

11. Cynthia took more than 200 _____, some with her camera and some using her phone.

12. On her African _____, Karen saw zebras, elephants, and lions.

© Saddleback Educational Publishing • www.sdlback.com
Common Core Skills & Strategies for Vocabulary: Level 7
CCSS: L.7.2b, L.7.4, L.7.4a, L.7.5, L.7.5b, RH.6-8.4, RST.6-8.4 127

NAME _____ DATE _____

GOVERNMENT WORDS 1

Directions: Unscramble the words that match the definitions. Then use the unscrambled words to complete the crossword puzzle. Item 4-Across has been done for you.

ACROSS

4. executive (ECEUTXIEV) — having the duty and power of putting laws into effect
6. _____ (REPBAMEL) — the introductory section of the Constitution
7. _____ (DANENSMEMT) — changes and additions to the Constitution
9. _____ (UCLJIADI) — the branch of government of which the courts are a part
11. _____ (TAMECDOR) — a member of one of the major political parties in the U.S.
13. _____ (VELSIELAGTI) — the branch of government responsible for passing laws
14. _____ (PIAMCEH) — to formally charge a public official with wrongdoing in office
15. _____ (GYANEC) — a governmental bureau that carries out a certain kind business
16. _____ (BAETCIN) — a group of official advisers and assistants to the president

DOWN

1. _____ (BYLTOSBI) — a person who tries to influence legislators in favor of some special interest
2. _____ (CETOLREAL) — having to do with an election or electors
3. _____ (PLIRBCEUAN) — a member of one of the major political parties in the U.S.
5. _____ (TTICOOINUSTN) — the fundamental body of laws governing the U.S.
8. _____ (ESTNEA) — the upper house of the U.S. Congress
10. _____ (NOESDICI) — a conclusion or judgment made by the Supreme Court
12. _____ (CETLE) — to choose by voting

128 CCSS: L.7.2b, L.7.4, L.7.4a, L.7.5, L.7.5b, RH.6-8.4, RST.6-8.4

NAME _____ DATE _____

GOVERNMENT WORDS 2

Directions: Use the crossword puzzle answers to correctly complete the sentences.

1. The _____ of the United States consists of seven articles.

2. Some 26 _____ have been made to the Constitution.

3. The Supreme Court is the highest body in the _____ branch.

4. The _____ office in the United States is held by the president.

5. Congress makes up the _____ branch of the federal government.

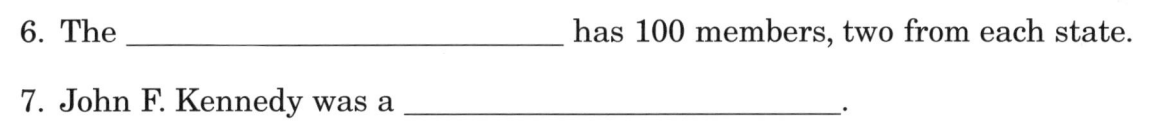

6. The _____ has 100 members, two from each state.

7. John F. Kennedy was a _____.

8. Ronald Reagan was a _____.

9. The _____ to the Constitution begins with the words "We the people of the United States."

10. Members of the _____ give the president information and advice.

11. The president is elected by members of the _____ college.

12. A _____ uses many methods to influence legislators on behalf of special interests.

13. The Supreme Court's job is to make _____ about important legal cases.

© Saddleback Educational Publishing • www.sdlback.com
Common Core Skills & Strategies for Vocabulary: Level 7   CCSS: L.7.2b, L.7.4, L.7.4a, L.7.5, L.7.5b, RH.6-8.4, RST.6-8.4   **129**

NAME _____ DATE _____

PARTY WORDS 1

Directions: Unscramble the words that match the definitions. Then use the unscrambled words to complete the crossword puzzle. Item 2-Across has been done for you.

ACROSS

2. ___occasion___ a special reason for a party
   (SOCANOCI)
7. _____ people who come to a party
   (SGSUTE)
8. _____ a lively celebration
   (LAGA)
10. _____ food and drink served at a party
    (STFEMREERSHN)
13. _____ what a band provides at a party
    (TNERETANINTEM)
14. _____ how to acquaint two strangers with each other
    (TRUNINODICOT)
15. _____ how people relate to each other at a party
    (TONITIRNEAC)
16. _____ the condition of being happy or diverted
    (MASEMEUNT)

DOWN

1. _____ friendly, informal talk between persons
   (NATCOVSERINO)
3. _____ a person who makes and serves food for a party
   (RETCARE)
4. _____ the one with whom you dance
   (RENPRAT)
5. _____ recognition of a special event with a party
   (BETCREILANO)
6. _____ an elaborate meal or feast
   (QUBAENT)
9. _____ food served before the main course
   (RESAZPEPIT)
11. _____ an important happening
    (NETEV)
12. _____ requiring elaborate dress and manners
    (RAFLOM)

NAME _____ DATE _____

PARTY WORDS 2

Directions: Use the crossword puzzle answers to correctly complete the sentences.

1. _____ at the afternoon party included appetizers and beverages.

2. _____ dress was required, so Richard rented a tuxedo.

3. A good _____ should provide each person with some information about the other.

4. As the party ended, Meg and Dylan were in the middle of a long _____.

5. Michelle's dance _____ knows all the latest steps.

6. The _____ for the party was Jeffrey's sixteenth birthday.

7. All of the _____ had a wonderful time at the party.

8. The _____ of Arielle's graduation lasted for three days.

9. The band, the singer, and the clown all provided _____ for the party guests.

10. The _____ table was adorned with fine linen and sparkling crystal.

11. About an hour before the main course, the _____ were served.

12. The food prepared by the young _____ was quite delicious.

© Saddleback Educational Publishing • www.sdlback.com
Common Core Skills & Strategies for Vocabulary: Level 7   CCSS: L.7.2b, L.7.4, L.7.4a, L.7.5, L.7.5b, RH.6-8.4, RST.6-8.4   131

Scope and Sequence

Student

Columns:
- Formal/Informal Language
- Dictionary Entries
- Denotation
- Connotation
- Euphemisms/Dysphemisms
- Pronunciation
- Silent Letters
- Syllabication
- Accent Marks
- Context Clues
- Variant Word Forms
- Compound Words
- Greek Roots
- Latin Roots
- Prefixes
- Suffixes
- Near Misses
- Synonyms: Nouns
- Synonyms: Verbs
- Synonyms: Adjectives

Scope and Sequence

Student

Columns:
- Synonyms: Adverbs
- Antonyms: Nouns
- Antonyms: Verbs
- Antonyms: Adjectives
- Antonyms: Adverbs
- Homophones
- Homographs
- Clipped Words
- Foreign Words
- Interpreting Idioms
- Exploring Big Words
- Shopping Words
- Law Words
- Building Words
- Space Words
- Health Words
- Business Words
- Travel Words
- Government Words
- Party Words

Common Core Skills & Strategies for Vocabulary: Level 7

ANSWER KEY

PAGE 2
A. 1. perceive
2. calculate
3. abolish
4. signify
5. perturb
6. massive
7. baffle
8. notable
9. tedious
10. quest
B. 1. b 3. a 5. c
2. c 4. a

PAGE 3
A. 1. handle
2. bugs
3. ditzy
4. chill
5. sleazy
6. hangout
7. batty
B. 1. melancholy
2. cheap
3. observe
4. refined
5. gab
6. dis

PAGE 4
A. 1. mentor 3. first
2. third 4. erudite
B. 1. adjourn
2. ballast
3. cyclone
4. demerit
5. erupt
6. fragile
7. genial
8. geology
9. heifer
10. inquiry
11. jazz
12. kidnap
13. lapel
14. lavish
15. matrimony
16. oblong
17. romance
18. sentiment
19. wary
20. yonder
21. zenith

PAGE 5
A. 1. The following words should be crossed out: mayfly, material, maze.
2. Answers will vary but might include mathematics, matriarch, matter, and matrix.
B. 1. between 3. will
2. forward 4. before
C. The following words should be circled: geezer, general, gelatin; plowshare, ploy, plummet, plow.

PAGE 6
A. 1. agonies
2. tomatoes
3. fathers-in-law
4. mice
5. thieves
6. radii
B. 1. write 3. gone
2. fed 4. sit
C. 1. most attractive
2. more bored
3. fewest
4. more colossal

PAGE 7
A. 1. omelet
2. octopi
3. larvae
4. tepee
5. levelled
6. gladioli
7. makeup
8. halleluiah
B. 1. e 3. d 5. f 7. c
2. b 4. g 6. a

PAGE 8
A. 1. N 4. N 7. P 10. N
2. P 5. P 8. N 11. P
3. P 6. N 9. P 12. N
B. 1. devise
2. assertive
3. crowd
4. accumulate
5. persuade
6. bold
7. custodian
8. aroma
9. emphasize
10. thin

PAGE 9
1. pig-headed
2. emotional
3. donation
4. abandon
5. help
6. special
7. third-world country
8. disabled
9. employee
10. soldier
11. cur
12. mansion
13. restroom

PAGE 10
Approximate answers:
1. Redolent because a pelargonium is a flower, and redolent refers to smell.
2. Qishm: Iran; Qiqihar: China
3. Mellifluous because the word means "melodious," whereas cacophonous means "harsh-sounding."
4. No; a boutique sells clothing, accessories, and gifts. Borscht is cold beet soup.
5. Progenitors because the words describe ancestors. Progeny refers to descendants.
6. An epicure because he or she appreciates fine food, whereas a gourmand will eat anything without discrimination.
7. Ameliorate because the word means "to improve"; exacerbate means "to make worse."

PAGE 11
Approximate answers:
1. No; a eulogy is a funeral oration, and a euglena is a microscopic organism.
2. They are all open land areas.
3. Greece
4. A coati is a small tree-dwelling, raccoonlike carnivore with a long flexible snout, found in Mexico and Central and South America. An agouti is a rabbit-sized nocturnal rodent with grizzled fur, found in tropical America. What they have in common is that they are both small land animals found in the Western Hemisphere. One difference is that the coati lives in trees, and the agouti does not.
5. Amiable, because an amiable child is friendly and pleasant, whereas an obstreperous one is disobedient and unpleasant.
6. You might give an octogenarian (a person in his or her eighties) a cymbidium (an orchid) on his or her birthday, Mother's Day, Father's Day, or any other special occasion.
7. No, because a tyro is a beginner and a virtuoso is an expert.

PAGE 12
A SOUNDS
1. back, began
2. basic, volcano
3. almost, falter
4. beware, square
5. hard, party
6. another, agree
E SOUNDS
1. empty, spell
2. secret, female
3. something, operate, safety
4. baker, camera
5. happen, item, weapon
I SOUNDS
1. insect, which
2. wire, describe
3. dirty, shirt
O SOUNDS
1. opera, problem
2. ocean, cargo
3. sound, eyebrow
4. voice, joyous
5. song, office
6. cookie, wooden
7. troop, bamboo
8. canyon, method

PAGE 13
A. U SOUNDS
1. funny, summer
2. January, human
3. bullfrog, cushion
4. prune, cruel
5. turtle, surface
B. 1. there 6. pillow
2. pie 7. sauerkraut
3. flown 8. hood
4. treasure 9. plowed
5. plead 10. enough

PAGE 14
A. SILENT LETTER / CROSS OUT
1. c inspect, color
2. h showing, happy
3. w wander, wilt
4. t water, patted
5. l flap, tassel
6. g gather, sugar
7. b buzz, amber
8. k broken, mark
9. p perhaps, important
B. 1. black 4. two, four, five,
2. heart   eight, nine
3. science 5. descend

PAGE 15
A. 1. buffet 4. mistletoe
2. croquet 5. wretched
3. khaki 6. adjoining
B. ACROSS: 1. sight 4. honest
5. batch 9. debtor
DOWN: 2. thigh 3. reign
5. bristle 6. cartridge
7. lacquer 8. midget

PAGE 16
A. 1. 2-SYLLABLE WORDS
block • ade
tal • low
or • chid
2. 3-SYLLABLE WORDS
ac • knowl • edge
bun • ga • low
o • ver • sight
com • e • dy
3. 4-SYLLABLE WORDS
con • tin • u • ous
mel • an • chol • y
af • fec • tion • ate
con • sid • er • ate
4. 5-SYLLABLE WORDS
dis • a • gree • a • ble
ge • o • log • i • cal
de • vel • op • men • tal
or • gan • i • za • tion

PAGE 16 (continued)
B. 1. ATlas
2. phenOMenon
3. COMplicate
4. irREGular

PAGE 17
A. 1. first   5. second
2. first   6. third
3. first   7. second
4. third   8. second

B. 1. contest (noun): accent first syllable
   contest (verb): accent second syllable
2. conduct (verb): accent second syllable
   conduct (noun): accent first syllable
3. replay (noun): accent first syllable
   replay (verb): accent second syllable
4. address (verb): accent second syllable
   address (noun): accent first syllable

PAGE 18
1. jimple: a
2. dipdop: c
3. krinskis: b
4. sloozed: a
5. schlimper: b
6. gairblue: c
7. flang: a
8. moglump: c

PAGE 19
1. a   2. b   3. c   4. c   5. a   6. c

PAGE 20
1. impulse   5. film
2. honesty   6. attempt
3. players   7. rainfall
4. search   8. position

PAGE 21
1. operate   6. injured
2. forces   7. perform
3. complain   8. fainted
4. contrasted   9. tempt
5. conquered   10. scorch

PAGE 22
1. peaceful   6. difficult
2. destitute   7. firm
3. speechless   8. simple
4. bashful   9. humble
5. hectic   10. leisurely

PAGE 23
1. approximately
2. reluctantly
3. thoroughly
4. cordially
5. formerly
6. fundamentally
7. partially
8. violently
9. never
10. continuously

PAGE 24
A. ACROSS: 4. creation
5. brutality   6. gland
7. solitude
DOWN: 1. accuracy
2. hostility   3. prestige
4. change

B. 1. gland   5. prestige
2. change   6. brutality
3. creation   7. hostility
4. solitude   8. accuracy

PAGE 25
Sentences will vary; check for correct use of the nouns.
1. affection
2. consideration
3. eternity
4. fearlessness
5. venom
6. turbulence
7. suspicion
8. sentiment
9. resident
10. punctuality
11. monotony

PAGE 26
A. ACROSS: 2. preferable
4. filtered   6. punctuated
8. dried
DOWN: 1. warranted
3. dimpled   5. dead
7. tied

B. 1. dead
2. preferable
3. dimpled
4. filtered
5. dried
6. punctuated

C. Sentences will vary; check for correct use of the adjectives.
1. believable
2. enjoyable
3. preferable

PAGE 27
Sentences will vary; check for correct use of the adjectives.
1. sustained or sustainable
2. warped
3. rejected
4. radiant
5. rebellious
6. recognizable
7. excellent
8. successful
9. modified
10. persistent
11. intentional or intended

PAGE 28
A. ACROSS: 3. consume   4. drape
5. rescue   6. hate
DOWN: 1. dramatize
2. depend   3. complicate

B. 1. rescue   5. depend
2. hate   6. complicate
3. consume   7. drape
4. dramatize

PAGE 29
Sentences will vary; check for correct use of the verb.
1. postpone
2. lubricate
3. convict
4. confront
5. correspond
6. develop
7. organize
8. penetrate
9. paralyze
10. narrate
11. represent

PAGE 30
A. 2. bare, dare, hare
3. ride, side, hide
4. pest, test, best
5. beak, leak, teak
6. boot, root, loot

B. 1. track, stack, black
2. creep, sleep, cheep
3. chill, still, grill
4. brake, flake, drake

PAGE 31
A. 2. flash, flag, fact
3. brain, blob, bold
4. pale, pant, parch
5. cart, core, creek
6. none, nail, neither

B. 1. plant, fort, cart (or plane, fore, care)
2. pang, tang, bang
3. form, norm, warm
4. tarp, seep, damp

C. Possible answers:
2. frame (or flame)
3. baste
4. bang
5. coat (or colt)
6. hung
7. posse (or prose)
8. line (or lice, like)

PAGE 32
A. 2. c, wristwatch
3. e, airport
4. i, outside
5. a, scarecrow
6. l, touchdown
7. d, waterfall
8. g, overbite
9. h, pancake
10. m, skyscraper
11. f, silverware
12. b, paperback
13. k, breakfast

B. Student art will vary.

PAGE 33
A. 1. tiptoe
2. cupboard
3. peppermint
4. spotlight
5. highchair
6. sweatshirt
7. windmill

B. ACROSS: 1. flashback
4. outfit   6. pigtail
7. dishpan
DOWN: 2. lifeguard
3. carpool   5. goldfish
6. postcard

PAGE 34
A. 1. headphone, d
2. footbridge, e
3. footnote, f
4. headlights or footlights, g
5. footprint, a
6. footstool, c
7. headline, b

B. ACROSS: 2. headhunter
5. Football   6. headband
DOWN: 1. headache
3. headquarters
4. footboard   5. footlocker

PAGE 35
1. headdresses
2. foothold
3. headboard
4. headfirst
5. footwear
6. headset
7. footsteps
8. footloose
9. headway
10. footpath
11. footrace
12. headlock

PAGE 36
A. 1. airtight
2. waterlily
3. airmail
4. waterlogged
5. airport
6. waterfall

B. ACROSS: 2. airwaves
4. watercolors   5. airsick
6. watermelon   7. waterline
DOWN: 1. waterfront
3. airbrush

PAGE 37
1. waterfowl
2. watermark
3. airsafe or airworthy
4. waterproof or water-repellent
5. airstrike
6. watercress
7. airborne
8. airplane
9. watertight
10. airspace
11. waterfall

Common Core Skills & Strategies for Vocabulary: Level 7

PAGE 38
A.
1. windbag, d
2. sunglasses, f
3. windsock, g
4. sundown, a
5. sunrise, b
6. windbreaker, c
7. sundial, e

B. ACROSS: 1. windstorms
4. sunburn 6. windsurfed
7. sustan 8. windshield
DOWN: 2. sunbonnet
3. sunroof 5. windfall

PAGE 39
1. windjammer
2. sunbeam
3. windchill
4. windmills
5. sunlamp
6. windpipe
7. sunbathe
8. sunfish
9. windblown
10. sunscreen
11. sunflower

PAGE 40
A. Answers will vary. Possible answers:

G or S	SAMPLE ANSWER
3. G	elephant
4. S	gem
5. G	bracelet
6. G	rose
7. S	color
8. S	fish

B. Answers can appear in any order.
foolish—absurd;
hobby—obsession;
glad—ecstatic;
entertain—enthrall;
apologize—atone;
influence—domination;
admire—adore;
disagree—oppose;
alone—isolated

PAGE 41
Sentences will vary; check for correct use of the words.
SCRAMBLED WORDS:
2. amuse   5. sprint
3. engaging 6. glum
4. respond

PAGE 42
1. prognosis
2. telegram
3. cardiologist
4. tricycle
5. symphony
6. paleolithic
7. epidemic
8. polyandry
9. microphone
10. phonics
11. cyclops
12. Democrat

PAGE 43
A.
1. d   3. e   5. a
2. c   4. f   6. b

B.
1. eye
2. fear of
3. god

C. Possible answers:
1. cinema
2. paralysis
3. maniac
4. anesthetist

PAGE 44
1. submarine
2. recognized
3. manuscript
4. cordial
5. recliner
6. pedestrians
7. donated
8. curable
9. marines
10. manufacturing
11. quadrupeds

PAGE 45
A.
1. move   4. faith
2. see   5. war
3. move   6. common

B. Possible answers:
1. altimeter
2. gratuitous
3. documentary
4. paternity

PAGE 46
1. prototype
2. polygamy
3. quintuplets
4. contraindicated
5. benefactor
6. comfort
7. extraordinary
8. octet
9. polynomial
10. benediction

PAGE 47
A.
1. self   4. million
2. not   5. around
3. false   6. small

B.
1. embraced   4. embroider
2. enclose   5. enchanted
3. embezzle   6. encourage

PAGE 48
1. vacancy
2. fortitude
3. childhood
4. racism
5. capitalization
6. honesty
7. pallor
8. bravery
9. standardization
10. pacifism
11. fervor

PAGE 49
A.
1. maternal
2. statuesque
3. circular
4. military
5. picturesque
6. popular
7. natural

B.
1. fearful
2. Turbulent
3. nervous
4. comatose
5. successful
6. glorious

PAGE 50
1. collision
2. expand
3. loose
4. adopt
5. pursue
6. personnel
7. finally
8. voracious
9. perpetuate
10. deprived
11. calendar

PAGE 51
A. ACROSS: 3. lose 5. perpetrate
7. peruse 8. collusion
DOWN: 1. colander
2. depraved 4. veracious
6. finely

B.
1. d
2. g
3. b
4. i
5. a
6. j
7. c
8. e
9. f
10. h

PAGE 52
2. e, cavity
3. a, dwelling
4. c, flattery
5. i, ban
6. d, exaggeration
7. h, glint
8. f, haste
9. g, hatred
10. j, instructor

PAGE 53
1. rucksack
2. magician
3. competitor
4. passion
5. siege
6. storm
7. vase
8. temptation
9. testimony

PAGE 54
A.
1. insult
2. assure
3. induce
4. waver
5. invalidate
6. admit
7. catch
8. toss
9. expel

B.
1. deserve, justify
2. choose, prefer
3. harass, victimize
4. untangle, untwist
5. burn, char
6. appraise, assess
7. handy, suitable
8. differ, digress
9. curve, bend

PAGE 55
A.
1. lead
2. examine
3. cover
4. punch
5. soil
6. surround

B. Possible answers:
1. nap
2. mark
3. stink
4. entice
5. affect

C. Sentences will vary. Check for correct use of the synonyms.

PAGE 56
1. d, genuine
2. g, aged
3. i, ambitious
4. a, irritated
5. e, flimsy
6. j, changeable
7. c, received
8. f, miniature
9. h, hardy
10. b, intellectual

PAGE 57
A.
1. fancy, showy
2. manly, male
3. loyal, dependable
4. dangerous, risky
5. unique, unusual
6. pictorial, scenic

B. Possible answers:
1. catching
2. female
3. tasty
4. rebellious
5. terrific
6. tiny

PAGE 58
A.
1. h   6. e
2. d   7. i
3. g   8. j
4. b   9. f
5. a   10. c

B. ACROSS: 3. gladly 6. surely
8. completely
DOWN: 1. seldom 2. clearly
4. honestly 5. eternally
7. roughly

PAGE 59
1. first, originally
2. totally, entirely
3. simply, utterly
4. blindly, mindlessly
5. very, quite
6. accidentally, mistakenly
7. extremely, greatly
8. unusually, remarkably

PAGE 60
A.
1. c   3. a   5. i   7. h
2. f   4. e   6. l   8. j
9. b   10. d   11. g   12. k

B.
1. vigor
2. toil
3. clarity
4. patriotism
5. evil
6. maturity
7. foreground
8. jollity

C. Sentences will vary; check for correct use of the antonyms.
1. unity
2. reason
3. gentleman
4. rashness

PAGE 61
A. Answers can be in any order.
1. attic / cellar
2. brightness / dullness
3. cowardice / heroism
4. assistance / hindrance
5. fairness / injustice
6. deflation / inflation
7. courtesy / disrespect
8. elimination / inclusion
9. decision / hesitation
10. punishment / pardon
11. firmness / flabbiness
12. employed / jobless
13. triviality / importance
14. laughter / weeping

B. ACROSS: 2. escape 5. gainer
6. clarity 7. defend
DOWN: 1. roughness
3. poverty 4. knowledge

PAGE 62
1. abbreviate
2. disconnect
3. convicted
4. welcome
5. repel
6. ignored
7. released
8. improved
9. loosened

PAGE 63
A.
1. arrive
2. freeze
3. include
4. submit
5. envy
6. approach
7. sell
8. forbid
9. mock
10. conceal

B. ACROSS: 2. wrinkle 4. quarrel
7. finish 8. simplify
DOWN: 1. harden 3. excite
5. reveal 6. hire

PAGE 64
A.
1. formal
2. passive
3. straight
4. cherished
5. proud
6. imaginary
7. crowded
8. alien

B.
1. resistant
2. delicate
3. elongated
4. lowered
5. comfortable
6. bound
7. harmless
8. optimistic

PAGE 65
A.
1. gloomy
2. external
3. common
4. copied
5. brief
6. irrational
7. unruly
8. able
9. unethical
10. adequate

B. ACROSS: 4. inactive 6. lying
7. coarse
DOWN: 1. stingy 2. parched
3. refined 5. moral

PAGE 66
A.
1. abruptly
2. foolishly
3. often
4. brightly
5. briskly
6. certainly
7. unhappily
8. accidentally
9. thoughtfully

B. ACROSS: 3. carefully 5. fully
6. gently 7. crazily
DOWN: 1. clearly 2. listlessly
4. rudely 5. fairly

PAGE 67
A. Pairs of adverbs can be in any order.
2. definitely, questionably
3. commonly, unusually
4. obscurely, famously
5. awkwardly, gracefully
6. sometimes, invariably

B. ACROSS: 1. unluckily
6. sourly 7. safely
8. invariably 9. slowly
DOWN: 2. cruelly
3. unclearly 4. commonly
5. passively

PAGE 68
A.
1. aloud   7. scent
2. cruise 8. mane
3. lye   9. won
4. bawl
5. fined
6. meat or mete

B. ACROSS: 2. complement
4. hymn 5. whose
7. moan 8. pore 9. chute
10. aweigh
DOWN: 1. holy 3. tee
5. weave 6. shown
8. pause

C. 1. (circle buoy, fur, and beach) The boy climbed up the fir tree and the beech tree.
2. (circle wee, fore, and flairs) After the accident, we set off four flares to get attention.

PAGE 69
A.
1. barred bard
2. barque bark
3. boll bowl
4. serial cereal
5. kernels for colonels
6. night knight
7. high hi

B.
1. fryer friar
2. hostile hostel
3. plait plate
4. prophet for profit
5. pale pail
6. seen scene

PAGE 70
A.
2. pine
3. compound
4. blow
5. fine
6. hide

B. Answer: origins
2. jar
3. pitcher
4. page
5. kind
6. down
7. fresh

PAGE 71
A.
1. bow: possible answer: a knot with loops in it
2. blue: the color of the sky
3. corps: a large military unit
4. hey: a cry used to attract attention
5. lessen: to minimize

B. 2–3. Answers will vary. Check students' sentences for correct use of the homographs.

PAGE 72
A.
1. automobile
2. coeducational student
3. trigonometry
4. delicatessen
5. centum
6. cucumber
7. submarine
8. periwig

B.
1. vet
2. typo
3. lunch
4. deb
5. doc
6. mod
7. pants
8. mums

PAGE 73
A. ACROSS: 3. coattails
4. scramble 5. distillery
6. spectacles 7. percolate
DOWN: 1. lubricate 2. gabble

B.
1. hackney
2. curiosity
3. moving picture
4. penitentiary
5. turnpike
6. university
7. promenade

PAGE 74
A. 1. a   3. h   5. d   7. g
   2. c   4. f   6. e   8. b
B. 1. named after Attabiya, a quarter in Baghdad
   2. after Jean Martinet, a 17th century French army officer
   3. after Rudolf Diesel, born in Paris of German parents, who improved the internal combustion engine
   4. after John Duns Scotus, whose once accepted writings were ridiculed in the 16th century
   5. after Joseph Guillotin, the 19th century French physician who invented it

PAGE 75
ACROSS: 3. bloomers   5. atlas
6. bowler   11. pasteurize
12. Friday
DOWN: 1. July
2. graham crackers
4. maverick   7. teddy bear
8. volt   9. jersey
10. May

PAGE 76
1. c   3. b   5. a   7. c
2. a   4. b   6. b

PAGE 77
1. a   4. j   7. d   10. e
2. g   5. i   8. b   11. k
3. h   6. f   9. c

PAGE 78
A. 1. a   3. b
   2. c   4. a
B. 1. b   3. d   5. a   7. h
   2. g   4. f   6. c   8. e

PAGE 79
1. carried on
2. drew a blank
3. dress down
4. looked up to
5. lost face
6. cut back
7. see eye to eye
8. take on
9. get ahead
10. kept at

PAGE 80
1. b   3. c   5. c   7. b
2. a   4. a   6. a   8. c

PAGE 81
1. c   3. b   5. a   7. a
2. a   4. b   6. c   8. b

PAGE 82
1. b   3. a   5. c   7. a
2. c   4. a   6. b   8. b

PAGE 83
A. 1. chickens
   2. feet
   3. heels
   4. hoop
   5. brain
B. 1. b   3. d   5. c
   2. a   4. e

PAGE 84
1. b   3. b   5. c   7. a
2. c   4. a   6. a   8. b

PAGE 85
1. hold a candle to, playing second fiddle
2. eating them out of house and home, lay down the law
3. take it easy, make ends meet
4. come clean, turned a deaf ear to
5. make up for, pull strings
6. hit the nail on the head, fall short
7. have it both ways, get away with

PAGE 86
1. aerobics
2. belated
3. barge
4. barnacles
5. brocade
6. ability
7. accelerate
8. absorb
9. accessory
10. adhere
11. buoyant
12. agenda

PAGE 87
Answers will vary. Check students' sentences for correct use of the words.

PAGE 88
1. disguise
2. civilian
3. carbonated
4. dubious
5. cabaret
6. dahlia
7. credence
8. defiance
9. depreciate
10. custody
11. dexterity
12. cognizant

PAGE 89
Answers will vary. Check students' sentences for correct use of the words.

PAGE 90
1. escapade
2. flaunt
3. earnest
4. exceed
5. firmament
6. fallible
7. fragment
8. elaborate
9. fauna
10. froth
11. ecstasy
12. emulate

PAGE 91
Sentences will vary, but confirm that assigned word has been used properly.

PAGE 92
1. grimace
2. goblet
3. genuflect
4. homage
5. headquarters
6. hearth
7. grandiose
8. gallant
9. heritage
10. harvest
11. garment

PAGE 93
Answers will vary. Check students' sentences for correct use of the words.

PAGE 94
1. jaguar
2. illusion
3. inexpensive
4. jiggle
5. jungle
6. jumbo
7. jargon
8. identical
9. inconsistent
10. juvenile
11. inhale

PAGE 95
Answers will vary. Check students' sentences for correct use of the words.

PAGE 96
1. literacy
2. kernel
3. leisure
4. kiosk
5. lacquer
6. lopsided
7. kaleidoscope
8. languid
9. kosher
10. keg
11. kindle

PAGE 97
Answers will vary. Check students' sentences for correct use of the words.

PAGE 98
1. martyr
2. nomadic
3. naive
4. modem
5. muffin
6. nudge
7. nozzle
8. Mildew
9. mahogany
10. menace
11. nonchalant
12. necessary

PAGE 99
Answers will vary. Check students' sentences for correct use of the words.

PAGE 100
1. posture
2. patriarch
3. octave
4. pedicure
5. omnivorous
6. ordeal
7. obituary
8. purpose
9. ottoman
10. prize
11. phantom
12. original

PAGE 101
Answers will vary. Check students' sentences for correct use of the words.

PAGE 102
1. repent
2. quince
3. quell
4. quad
5. redeem
6. quota
7. rampage
8. quake
9. reverse
10. queasy
11. rupture

PAGE 103
Answers will vary. Check students' sentences for correct use of the words.

PAGE 104
1. temerity
2. tactful
3. triceps
4. sacrifice
5. smear
6. stiff
7. temper
8. silhouette
9. swelter
10. spare
11. thorn
12. segment

PAGE 105
Answers will vary. Check students' sentences for correct use of the words.

PAGE 106
1. varnish
2. unaccompanied
3. unkempt
4. ulcer
5. vulgar
6. vivid
7. undisciplined
8. vicinity
9. unsound
10. valid
11. utter

PAGE 107
Answers will vary. Check students' sentences for correct use of the words.

PAGE 108
1. whiff
2. X-axis
3. xerothermic
4. xenophobe
5. wharf
6. wad
7. wade
8. Xylem
9. xerography
10. wallet
11. warble

PAGE 109
Answers will vary. Check students' sentences for correct use of the words.

PAGE 110
1. yogurt
2. yearling
3. yoga
4. yacht
5. yam
6. zodiac
7. zealot
8. yelp
9. zenith
10. zori
11. zinnia

PAGE 111
Answers will vary. Check students' sentences for correct use of the words.

PAGE 112
1. because a fakir is a Hindu or Muslim holy person who is a beggar, and a fedora is a hat that such a beggar would not be able to afford
2. at its perigee because then the moon is closest to the earth
3. because an ascetic is someone who has chosen not to have pleasure or comforts, and silk is a luxury cloth
4. because a buccaneer is a pirate and a brigantine is a type of ship
5. because an impostor would be hiding his identity, and going incognito would accomplish this purpose
6. rhinestones, because lodestones are naturally magnetized pieces of magnetite, an iron ore, not a stone used in jewelry
7. because a semaphore is a tower with movable arms used to signal railroad trains
8. a jennet because it is a small Spanish horse

PAGE 113
1. a lectern because a teacher often gives a lecture, and a lectern is a piece of furniture that can hold notes and a microphone, whereas legerdemain is the use of trickery or magic
2. rectitude because it is honesty and goodness in principles and conduct, whereas iniquity is great evil or injustice
3. a bellicose person because such a person would be likely to pick a fight, whereas a comatose person is in a coma
4. a loquacious person because such a person is talkative, whereas a mendacious person tells lies
5. an adjustable bed because such a bed can move up and down and bend to make the patient more comfortable; a bed would not be considered reversible
6. in an agrarian setting, because the bobolink, a bird, is more likely to be found in the country than in the city
7. a person who had versatility because such a person would be able to do many different tasks, whereas someone who had culpability would be guilty of some wrongdoing

PAGE 114
ACROSS:
2. compare
6. discount
9. ingredients
10. label
11. factory
12. comparison
13. sale
14. credit
16. exchange
17. cosmetics
18. guarantee

DOWN:
1. quality
3. pricetag
4. dry clean
5. lightweight
7. department
8. price
10. lingerie
15. large

PAGE 115
1. ingredients
2. factory
3. label
4. department
5. dry clean
6. discount
7. exchange
8. quality
9. cosmetics
10. credit
11. pricetag, price
12. sale

PAGE 116
ACROSS:
2. swear
6. jury
7. testify
9. parole
10. sentence
11. trial
14. summation
15. defendant
16. truth
17. argue
18. defense

DOWN:
1. plaintiff
3. witness
4. probation
5. prosecution
6. justice
8. verdict
12. attorney
13. judge

PAGE 117
1. witness
2. probation
3. verdict
4. trial
5. jury
6. prosecution
7. defendant
8. defense
9. prosecution
10. truth
11. judge
12. justice

PAGE 118
ACROSS:
1. permits
5. landscaping
6. irrigation
10. bulldozer
11. construction
12. drywall
14. foundation
15. architect

DOWN:
2. shingles
3. patio
4. electrician
7. plumber
8. concrete
9. contractor
13. blueprint

PAGE 119
1. landscaping
2. irrigation
3. shingles
4. blueprint
5. architect
6. patio
7. plumber
8. permits
9. concrete
10. electrician
11. Construction
12. contractor

PAGE 120
ACROSS:
2. propulsion
6. rocket
7. interstellar
8. astronaut
9. orbit
10. launch
12. infinity
14. moon
16. satellite
17. quarks

DOWN:
1. spacecraft
3. interplanetary
4. galaxy
5. gravity
11. cosmos
13. planet
15. pulsar

PAGE 121
1. astronaut
2. rocket
3. launch
4. orbit
5. gravity
6. galaxy
7. planet
8. moon
9. interstellar
10. Interplanetary
11. pulsar
12. quark

PAGE 122
ACROSS:
- 4. muscular
- 6. stress
- 9. vitamin
- 10. capillary
- 13. fiber
- 14. lipid
- 15. treatment
- 16. heartbeat

DOWN:
- 1. cardiovascular
- 2. nutrition
- 3. insomnia
- 4. mineral
- 5. carbohydrates
- 7. fatigue
- 8. metabolism
- 11. stretch
- 12. symptom

PAGE 123
- 1. vitamin
- 2. carbohydrates
- 3. muscular
- 4. nutrition
- 5. stretch
- 6. heartbeat
- 7. stress
- 8. fatigue
- 9. insomnia
- 10. symptom
- 11. metabolism
- 12. treatment

PAGE 124
ACROSS:
- 1. cubicle
- 4. assistant
- 7. client
- 8. employee
- 12. secretary
- 13. overtime
- 14. deadline
- 15. meeting

DOWN:
- 2. benefits
- 3. employer
- 5. salary
- 6. committee
- 7. conference
- 9. vacation
- 10. president
- 11. project

PAGE 125
- 1. vacation
- 2. client
- 3. committee
- 4. employee
- 5. project
- 6. deadline
- 7. employer
- 8. benefits
- 9. salary
- 10. overtime
- 11. secretary
- 12. president

PAGE 126
ACROSS:
- 1. tropical
- 3. safari
- 4. passport
- 7. restaurant
- 9. accommodations
- 12. hotel
- 13. sightseeing
- 15. pyramids
- 16. souvenir
- 17. translate

DOWN:
- 2. airfare
- 3. suitcase
- 5. transportation
- 6. security
- 8. photographs
- 10. museum
- 11. guide
- 14. tourist

PAGE 127
- 1. pyramids
- 2. transportation
- 3. passport
- 4. security
- 5. airfare
- 6. suitcase
- 7. hotel
- 8. sightseeing
- 9. translate
- 10. souvenir
- 11. photographs
- 12. safari

PAGE 128
ACROSS:
- 4. executive
- 6. preamble
- 7. amendments
- 9. judicial
- 11. Democrat
- 13. legislative
- 14. impeach
- 15. agency
- 16. cabinet

DOWN:
- 1. lobbyist
- 2. electoral
- 3. Republican
- 5. Constitution
- 8. Senate
- 10. decision
- 12. elect

PAGE 129
- 1. Constitution
- 2. amendments
- 3. judicial
- 4. executive
- 5. legislative
- 6. Senate
- 7. Democrat
- 8. Republican
- 9. preamble
- 10. cabinet
- 11. electoral
- 12. lobbyist
- 13. decisions

PAGE 130
ACROSS:
- 2. occasion
- 7. guests
- 8. gala
- 10. refreshments
- 13. entertainment
- 14. introduction
- 15. interaction
- 16. amusement

DOWN:
- 1. conversation
- 3. caterer
- 4. partner
- 5. celebration
- 6. banquet
- 9. appetizers
- 11. event
- 12. formal

PAGE 131
- 1. Refreshments
- 2. Formal
- 3. introduction
- 4. interaction or conversation
- 5. partner
- 6. occasion
- 7. guests
- 8. celebration
- 9. entertainment
- 10. banquet
- 11. appetizers
- 12. caterer